ALEKSANDR BLOK

Aleksandr Blok

Selected Poems

translated from the Russian
by Jon Stallworthy and Peter France

CARCANET

First published in 1970 by Eyre and Spottiswoode.

This edition published in Great Britain in 2000 by
Carcanet Press Limited
4th Floor, Conavon Court
12-16 Blackfriars Street
Manchester M3 5BQ

A CIP catalogue record for this book
is available from the British Library.

ISBN 1 85754 473 0

The publisher acknowledges financial
assistance from the Arts Council of England.

Set in 10pt Garamond Simoncini by Bryan Williamson, Frome
Printed and bound by Antony Rowe Ltd, Eastbourne

Contents

5

Acknowledgements

This book, like many another, owes its inception to Sir Maurice Bowra, who in a tutorial on Yeats's poetry introduced the unknown name of Aleksandr Blok. To him and to Max Hayward, who provided the literal version of 'The Twelve', is owed a special debt of gratitude. Thanks are also due to Vaughan James, Sergei Hackel, and Robin Milner-Gulland, for advice on specific points of interpretation.

Other acknowledgements are due to the editors of the following periodicals in which some of these poems first appeared: *The Cambridge Review, The Critical Quarterly, The Guardian, The London Magazine, The Oxford Magazine, Solstice, Spectator, Sussex Poetry*, and *The Times Literary Supplement*; also to the BBC Third Programme.

Introduction

Aleksandr Blok, who lived from 1880 to 1921, is unquestionably one of Russia's greatest poets. The most prominent of the Russian symbolists, but also the author of the greatest poem of the Bolshevik Revolution, 'The Twelve', he was a conspicuous, often controversial figure, but also a great influence on some of the constellation of slightly younger poets – Akhmatova, Tsvetaeva, Mandelstam – who are now so well-known in the West. Pasternak wrote of him in 1956: 'His fame is not due to curricula, he lives eternally outside all schools and systems, he is not the work of men's hands, and was imposed on us by no one. He is free as the wind.'

Even so, Blok has not really received his due in the English-speaking world. In 1943, it is true, Sir Maurice Bowra introduced him eloquently to a wide British public in his *Heritage of Symbolism*, and since then there have been a fair number of books about him in English, notably Avril Pyman's great two-volume *Life of Aleksandr Blok* (OUP, 1979–80), together with the more informal, brief *Aleksandr Blok: A Life* (Carcanet, 1996), translated by Robyn Marsack from the French of Nina Berberova. The problem lies, inevitably, in the translation of the poetry.

Translators have clustered around 'The Twelve'; Avril Pyman, in her bilingual edition (University of Durham Press, 1989) lists seventeen preceding translations, from the almost contemporaneous version by C. Bechofer to the fine Scots rendering by Sydney Goodsir Smith. For all its greatness, though, 'The Twelve' is not all of Blok, and his other work is much less well-represented in English. When the present selection came out in 1970, it was the first volume to offer a reasonably comprehensive view. Subsequently came a larger *Selected Poems*, translated by Alex Millar, published in Moscow in 1981, and not easily available. Fine translations have also appeared in journals, of course, but Blok had not been offered to the English-speaking public in anything like the range of good translations attracted by Mandelstam or Akhmatova. All this makes it seem worthwhile to reissue at the beginning of the century a lightly revised edition of our original volume, which has long been out of print.

Our aim, now as in 1970, is to present in one volume a large enough collection of translations to give the English-speaking reader some impression of Blok's scope and his distinctive voice. In working we tried to follow the example set by those distinguished teams in which someone who was primarily a poet worked with someone who was primarily a scholar, hoping thereby to avoid some of the pitfalls that lie in wait for the translator of poetry who is not equally translator and poet. Some have argued that such a method is doomed to produce Frankensteinian monsters; we can only say that the proof of the pudding must be in the eating.

We are all too aware of the gaps that often separate Blok's poems from ours. Nevertheless, in so far as translators have to choose between what used to be called fidelity and beauty, we aimed for beauty, trying to produce poems which could stand by themselves in the late twentieth century, even if this meant doing violence on occasion to the patterns, rhythms, rhymes and (occasionally) meaning of the Russian poems. Not that we ever parted company from Blok lightheartedly; indeed, we sometimes found ourselves at odds, with one of us aspiring – often in vain – to find in English the sounds and rhythms of the original, and the other quite rightly insisting that doing justice to Blok meant above all producing poems that *worked*.

Translating Russian poetry today presents problems that did not exist for earlier generations. The reason is simply this: English poetry has largely broken with the formal prosody and rhetoric which flourished until early in the twentieth century, whereas today many Russian poets still write – very successfully – in what is recognizably the poetic tradition of the nineteenth century. Blok was in many respects a pioneer of poetic form, but to modern Western ears, his poems would in all likelihood sound bombastic or ridiculous if one were to reproduce in translation their heavy tonic stresses, strong effects of symmetry, regularity of rhyme and metre, and frequently archaic diction. Even if we did not entirely avoid these traps in our work, we tried at least to loosen and dislocate the prosodic regularity and the flow of eloquence when they ran too great a risk of deterring the English-speaking reader. But still we hope to have rendered something of Blok's famous music, which is easy to enthuse about, hard to analyse, but certainly not unconnected with the supple use of traditional verse forms. To have abandoned this altogether, in favour of the freer forms commonly used in verse translation today, would have given a distorted picture of the variety and range of Blok's poetry, where formality combines with freedom, elevated language with vulgarity, public discourse with personal meditation and with song.

This is how we worked together: first, PF would send JS a literal line-by-line prose version of a poem, with an approximate metrical score, notes on rhyme and rhythm, tone, vocabulary, repetitions, ambiguities of meaning, and so on, thus:

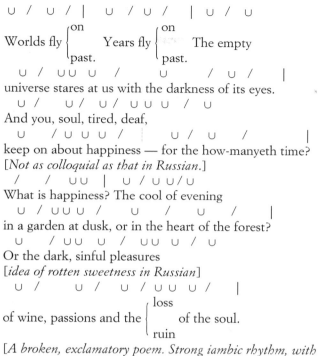

```
U / U / |   U / U /   | U / U
```
Worlds fly {on past.   Years fly {on past.   The empty
```
 U /  UU  U   /      U      /  U /      |
```
universe stares at us with the darkness of its eyes.
```
 U /   U /  U /  UU U  /  U
```
And you, soul, tired, deaf,
```
 U    / U U U /  |    U / U    /        |
```
keep on about happiness — for the how-manyeth time?
[*Not as colloquial as that in Russian.*]
```
 /   /   UU  |  U / UU/U
```
What is happiness? The cool of evening
```
 U / UUU /   U   /   U   /     |
```
in a garden at dusk, or in the heart of the forest?
```
 U   / UU  U  / UU U / U
```
Or the dark, sinful pleasures
[*idea of rotten sweetness in Russian*]
```
 U /    U /  U / UU U /   |
```
of wine, passions and the { loss ruin   of the soul.

[*A broken, exclamatory poem. Strong iambic rhythm, with
some irregularity. ABAB.*]

This JS endeavoured to coax into the diction and rhythms of a twen-
tieth-century English poem, with as little alteration as possible:

World fly past. Years fly past. The empty
universe darkly looks down on us.
And you, my shuttered soul, deafened and weary
keep on about happiness, happiness.

What's happiness? The undertones of twilight
in a cooling garden or a forest aisle;
forbidden entertainment, the dark delights
of liquor, lust, and the soul's betrayal?

Assuming that the general movement and tone of the English poem
were a fair reflection of the Russian (as was not always the case), PF
would offer specific criticisms:

Line 5.   'undertones' seems a little thought-out. In Russian it's a
simple, even banal image.

11

Line 6.   'aisle' sounds too religious. Blok's forest is thicker and wilder.

Line 6.   'cooling' — 'cool'? 'Cooling garden' sounds distinctly odd.

JS would try again:

What's happiness? The cool hour of twilight
in a fading garden or a forest trail;

This dialogue could continue for several exchanges, with perhaps a reading aloud of the Russian in between to give JS a better idea of the sound he was striving for.

Of the many hundreds of poems which Blok wrote, this volume contains only fifty. We naturally picked the poems we liked best or those which seemed to go best into English. But at the same time we hope to have given a fair selection from Blok's various themes and styles, enough to enable the reader to see in outline the development of his writing from 1900 to 1918. We only regret that we were not able to include any of his plays or any of his dazzling lyrical essays. Like all anthologizers, we must hope that readers will be sufficiently taken by what they read here to want to find out more by reading such works as Avril Pyman's biography, by seeking out other translations, and, ideally, by learning enough Russian to read this great poet in the original.

Blok once wrote that from 1897 on all his lyrical verse could be regarded as a diary. He tried to get away from this self-centred lyricism in his plays and in his long poem 'Retribution', but essentially he remained a lyric poet in the Romantic tradition. Almost all the poems in this volume are an expression of his thoughts and emotions at the time of writing. But this diary is not self-explanatory, still less the brief selection given here; one understands it better if one knows something of the life of the diarist.

Aleksandr Aleksandrovich Blok was born in 1880. His mother's family, which influenced him much more than his father's side, were old-fashioned liberal intellectuals. His grandfather was Rector of St Petersburg University; his grandmother, who 'was capable of rejoicing simply in sunshine and fine weather', spent much of her time translating. So too did her three daughters; Blok's autobiographical sketch of 1915 is full of these translations from Rousseau, Dickens, Beecher Stowe, Huxley, and many others. The whole family lived for the word; as Blok put it, 'to use Verlaine's terms, *eloquence* reigned supreme in my family; only my mother experienced constant disquiet and uneasiness about the new, and encouraged my aspirations to *music*.' Blok's father was quite different; in this well-bred family he appeared a sombre Byronic outsider. His marriage with Blok's mother did not last; after their divorce he lived out a tormented life teaching at the University of Warsaw, while she married an amiable army officer.

In what he later called the 'years of stagnation', Blok had a sheltered childhood, divided between St Petersburg (mainly military barracks) and the family's country estate at the little village of Shakhmatovo near Moscow, where he continued to spend the summer months for most of his life. The old-world culture of his family protected him from new philosophy and poetry until he was twenty; he later wrote: 'I owe a life-long debt to dear old-fashioned "eloquence", in that literature for me did not begin with Verlaine and the decadents.' His first models were the great poets of the early nineteenth century. The love of eloquence also showed itself in his early interest in the theatre; he had ideas of being an actor and played parts (such as Hamlet) in amateur theatricals in and around Shakhmatovo. On leaving school, he entered the Faculty of Law at St Petersburg but soon transferred to the Faculty of Letters. 'The University,' he later wrote, 'did not play a particularly important part in my life.'

The really important events of his youth were the mystical experiences which inspired his first book of verse. It is hard to give a precise description of these experiences, which were to determine the whole course of his life. They all centre round the Beautiful Lady, who appears as a female figure of perfection and harmony. On rare occasions she might reveal herself openly to men, as she did to Blok in 1901; otherwise they might glimpse her fleetingly in nature (the landscapes of Shakhmatovo) or in the features of women. There was hope too that she might manifest herself not just to the individual, but in the working of history, bringing a new life and a new harmony with the cosmos to a society which had lost touch with the Spirit of Music. Later, Blok linked her music and the elemental music of the Russian people.

In many ways his ideas were influenced by the philosopher Vladimir Solovyov (1853–1900), whose poems, he says, took possession of his entire being in the summer of 1901. But whereas for Solovyov there was a connection between Sophia, the Divine Wisdom, and Christ, Blok's poems of this period, though they are full of the imagery of churches and icons, make no mention of Christ. In 1904 he wrote to a Christian friend: 'Nothing – and this is final – will ever make me turn to Christ for a cure. I do not know Him and have never known Him.' In any case Blok's mystical experiences preceded his reading of

Solovyov. As he wrote in his autobiography, 'Up to this time the mysticism which had permeated the atmosphere of the turn of the century had been almost incomprehensible to me. I was disturbed by signs which I saw in nature [see 'A Red Glow in the Sky'], but I thought this was all "subjective" and kept it carefully hidden from everyone.' Solovyov simply confirmed his belief in the objective reality of this supernatural being and in the existence of what he called 'other worlds'. This belief never left him, however far he seemed to depart from it in later years.

Nevertheless there is a disquieting ambiguity about these poems and a striking parallelism between Blok's relation with his Beautiful Lady and the ups and downs of his courtship of Lyubov Dmitrievna Mendeleeva, who was to become his wife in the summer of 1903. He himself, when he later wrote a commentary on his early verse, interpreted many poems on two levels, the 'psychological' and the 'mystical'. As he felt more or less close to the woman, so the Beautiful Lady seemed to approach or recede. It is little wonder that certain critics have tended to treat the Beautiful Lady simply as a product of Blok's quite human experiences in love. Although he would certainly have rejected any such simple interpretation, convinced as he was of the reality of other worlds, he did not make any clear distinction between Lyubov Dmitrievna and the Beautiful Lady. The confusion was increased by his friends Sergei Solovyov (nephew of the philosopher) and Andrei Bely (one of the pillars of Russian symbolism), who built up a rather ridiculous mystical cult round Blok and his wife; hence, in part his subsequent hostility to 'mystical charlatans'.

At all events, the Beautiful Lady, whether human or divine, was the object of a great number of poems between 1901 and 1903, many of them prayer-like expressions of Blok's ecstasy, expectation or hope (see 'I Seek Salvation', 'The Intellect cannot Measure the Divine', and 'I Enter the Dark Church Slowly'). But all the time in these poems there is a sense of anguish and foreboding, a fear that the Beautiful Lady will abandon him or 'change her shape' (see 'I Sense Your Coming'). Blok was heavily burdened with the despairing irony which seemed to him to be one of the great curses of the intelligentsia of his time. Two themes express this most clearly, that of the double and that of the harlequinade, both of them tending to undermine or deform the ideal, turning the poet into a play-actor and substituting for the Beautiful Lady a beautiful doll, Astarte, the goddess of sex (and for Blok sex was something demonic, radically opposed to the vision of the Beautiful Lady). All these forebodings were borne out in the years following 1902. This is how he described the process:

14

The whole pattern of experience is totally transformed with the beginning of the 'antithesis' or 'change of feature', which had been foreseen from the very beginning of the 'thesis'. The events which bear witness to this are the following.

As if jealous of the lonely prophet's vision of the Dawn Radiance, someone suddenly breaks the golden thread of flowering miracles; the blade of the translucent sword is dimmed and is no longer felt in the heart. The worlds, which were formerly shot through with golden light, lose their purple hue; as if through a broken dam, a universal lilac-blue twilight bursts in, to the heartrending accompaniment of violins and refrains like gipsy songs. If I were painting a picture I should convey the experience of the moment in this way: in the lilac twilight of the vast world rocks a huge white catafalque and on it lies a dead doll with a face vaguely resembling what was once glimpsed among the roses of heaven. . . . The man who experiences all this is no longer alone; he is full of many demons (otherwise known as 'doubles') which the caprices of his evil creative will form into ever-changing groups of conspirators. At every moment, with the help of these conspirators, he hides some part of his soul from himself. Thanks to his net of deceit – which is all the more skilful, the more enchanting is the surrounding lilac twilight – he manages to make of each of the demons a weapon for himself, to bind with a pact each of the doubles; they all roam through the lilac worlds and, obedient to his will, fetch the most precious things: one brings the thundercloud, a second the sighing of the sea, a third the amethyst, a fourth the sacred beetle, the winged eye. All this their master throws into the cauldron of his *artistic creation* and at last, with the help of enchantments, he attains – for his amazement and amusement – the unknown object of his searches – a beautiful doll.

This passage, taken from Blok's lyrical article of 1910, 'On the Present State of Russian Symbolism', gives a vivid picture of his Faustian conception of art. The poet, having lost the Beautiful Lady, is left with the artificial hell of art (see 'To the Muse'). The whole human world is his to make beautiful poems, his witchcraft can conjure up shapes (the Stranger, the Snow Maiden) which take the place of the Beautiful Lady for a moment, but are in fact completely opposed to her. However it may seem to the audience (see 'The Artist'), to the poet art is a poor compensation for his lost communion.

In all this there is no question of a loss of faith in the Beautiful Lady. Although the poet, with his damned irony, may no longer be worthy to write about her, she continues to exist and her existence determines the poet's feeling of loss and his hope for the future. Indeed Blok himself, although he was aware of what he called the technical superiority of his later poems, said more than once towards the end of his life that his early poems were his most important writings. We may think differently, but we cannot write off the Beautiful Lady as mere meaningless dreaming.

From 1903, then, Blok entered the world of art and the world of men. One of the first changes was that poems set in the country were succeeded by poems of St Petersburg, the weird city of Dostoevsky, which Blok loved and hated as a symbol of the artificial hell he now lived in. Many poems reflect his wanderings in the backstreets and the suburbs; these usually stress the horror and unreality of the urban landscape (see 'Illusion'); less frequently there is a note of social concern, as in 'The Factory'. Like many intellectuals, he was enthusiastic about the Revolution of 1905 and is reported to have carried a red flag in a demonstration – a far cry from his disdain for politics in 1901. He at first saw in the Revolution a manifestation of the Beautiful Lady in history – at this time he was haunted by the image of her sailing in from the sea (see 'A Girl was Singing'). He was, however, quickly disillusioned and depressed by the backlash of reaction, and subsequently talked of the Revolution of 1905 as he talked of the Stranger – an illusion or doll conjured up to mask the void, but failing to bring any real transformation.

There followed a bleak period, in which Blok's relations with his wife seem to have deteriorated and in which more than ever he took refuge in drink (see 'The Stranger'), often with his friend the 'mystical anarchist' Chulkov, who described him at this time as 'the personification of catastrophe, total negation'. Blok's world was a world of absolutes, and now it was absolute desolation. But at the same time a new theme was beginning to sound in his poetry, a theme which seemed to offer a hope of escape from the nightmare of St Petersburg, the theme of the poor wanderer on the open road of Russia (see 'Autumn Freedom' and 'Russia'). A lyrical article of 1906 describes the vagabonds who are carried out of the deathly city in a whirling snowstorm; they may look like hopeless exiles, says Blok, 'but they are blessed creatures. Orphaned of their own will and condemning themselves to endless wandering, they walk on wherever the road leads them. And they look straight ahead along the stony track over the limitless plains of Russia.' He was beginning to see the only hope for the doomed city-dwelling intellectuals in the acceptance of the poverty and humiliation of vagabond Russia.

In the same year (1906), Blok made his first attempt to break out of the desperate circle of lyricism by writing plays. As a young man he had been interested in acting (one of his recurring horrors was that of being no more than an actor in life) and from 1906 until the end of his life he attached a great deal of importance to the theatre, regarding it as an art-form which enabled the writer to make contact with other people and a reality outside himself. He wrote half a dozen plays in all and a great number of critical articles and reviews. In spite of this, his plays, though fascinating and often very attractive, remain essentially personal statements, exploiting the themes of his verse in a way which is not convincingly dramatic. His first play, *The Puppet Show*, in which he mocked both himself and his 'mystical' contemporaries, was put on by the experimental company directed by Meyerhold. Blok was closely involved in the production and saw a good deal of the company. In particular he was captivated by the actress N.N. Volokhova, who inspired a great series of lyric poems in 1907.

At this period Blok gave contemporaries the impression of a tragic actor, playing a part of fatal passion. With Volokhova he felt that he was surrendering himself to the elements, first to the snowstorm (see 'Caught in the Blizzard') and later to the wild music of the gipsy, which was to continue to resound through his poems as the music of desperate ecstasy (see 'O what is the Setting Sun's Radiance' and 'Accordeon'). There is nothing in common between the Snow Maiden (as he called her) and the Beautiful Lady. The Snow Maiden is another of the dolls which take the place of the original vision, a comet like the Stranger, bringing not reality, harmony, and life, but demonic sex, wild music, unreality, and death – or, if not death, a sort of oblivion, which will purge away the old tedium and leave the possibility of a new life (see 'O Spring without End'). After the snowstorm the gipsy music leads out to the open spaces of Russia.

In this respect, 1908 was a crucial year for Blok. Becoming increasingly aware, like so many Russian intellectuals before the Revolution, of the great gap separating the intelligentsia and the Russian people, he tried to break out of his artificial world towards a closer contact with the people. At this time he wrote to Bely: 'I am healthy and simple, I am becoming ever simpler, as simple as I can.' Rejecting the more esoteric sides of symbolism, he tried to reconcile the two enemy camps of symbolism and realism. He felt dissatisfied, too, with the *commedia del'arte* theories of Meyerhold, in whose company his wife was acting; against them he placed himself rather in the great line of Russian writers for whom writing was no game, but a serious attempt to communicate matters of vital importance. Indeed, Blok saw the poet's task as one of almost suicidal sincerity; his duty was to sacrifice himself, burn himself out (see 'Hard to be Moving among Them'). His latest play, *The Song of Fate*, he wanted produced not by Meyerhold, but by the realist Stanislavsky, and wrote to Stanislavsky to explain his position:

> This is how I see my theme, the theme of Russia (in particular the question of the intelligentsia and the people). I consciously and irrevocably *dedicate my life* to this theme. More and more clearly I come to see that it is the most important, the most vital and the most real of questions. I have been approaching this question for a long time, from the beginning of my conscious life, and I *know* that my road in its basic aspiration is as straight and as purposeful as an arrow.

Naturally Blok did not follow this road unwaveringly, but from 1908 Russia became a major theme in his writing. He now felt it his duty to take more part in public life, notably by way of journalism and lecturing. In 1908 he developed his ideas on the fate of the intelligentsia in a resounding lecture, 'The People and the Intelligentsia', which calls his fellow-intellectuals to a sense of reality and ends on a prophecy of doom:

> Gogol and many other Russian writers liked to imagine Russia as the embodiment of calm and sleep. But this sleep is ending; the calm is giving way to a distant and growing roar, quite unlike the confused roar of the city.
> Gogol also imagined Russia as a racing troika. 'Russia, whither are you flying? Answer!' But there is no answer – only the 'marvellous ringing of the troika bell'.
> The roar, which is growing so quickly that each year we hear it more closely, is the 'marvellous ringing' of the troika bell. What if the troika, round which 'the torn air thunders and turns to wind', is flying straight at us?

The roar of coming events and the prophecy of disaster sounded ever more clearly in Blok's poems – and perhaps most compellingly of all in 'On the Field of Kulikovo'.

However, although he might strive for a greater simplicity and a new realism, these did not come easily to him. It is true that he was naturally simpler and less intellectual than many of his friends (he found great satisfaction in working on the estate at Shakhmatovo), but his longing for an uncomplicated life was constantly contradicted by inner despair at his state of spiritual abandonment and repulsion in the face of the society he lived in. This was notably the case in 1909, when

18

he gave up journalism and lecturing and visited Italy with his wife. His visit only strengthened his disgust with post-Renaissance Western civilization (see 'Ravenna' and 'Florence'). A letter to his mother from Milan catches the mood of desolation and the flickering hope in Russia:

> More than ever I see that never until my dying day shall I accept or submit to anything in contemporary life. Its shameful form inspires only disgust in me. Nothing can be changed now – no revolution will change it. . . . I love only art, children, and death. Russia is for me as before – a lyrical force. In fact it does not exist, never has and never will. I have been reading *War and Peace* for a long time and have re-read almost all of Pushkin's prose. That does exist.

This note continued to sound in Blok's writing in the years which followed. Many of the poems written between 1908 and 1914 record both a disgust with the world and a horror at his own condition. To a certain extent, too, he remained the poet of the drunken orgy, the gipsy dance, and the ecstasies of despair (see 'I am Nailed to a Bar with Liquor'). On the other hand, the reference to Pushkin and Tolstoy in the letter quoted above reflects his attempt to develop a clear, realistic way of looking at his situation. In 1910 in particular he seems to have discovered a new strength; this found expression on one level in the cult of physical fitness and on another in the long and unfinished poem 'Retribution', which occupied him in 1910 and 1911. His aim here was to write something more epic than lyrical, setting his own individual fate in the context of Russian history since 1880. Those sections of the poem which he did complete are impressive; he handles Pushkin's classical iambic metre with a firm hand and evokes episodes of private and public history with great power. Nevertheless, one may doubt whether Blok was really the man for such an undertaking. Incapable of throwing off the 'curse' of lyricism, he was essentially the poet of the short poem, recording like a seismograph his own internal tremors. Even so, 'Retribution' shows that, without in any way renouncing the Romantic or Symbolist belief that the artist's task is above all to seek the promised land, Blok had developed a formidable ability to evoke life as it is. This we see in many other poems of this period. In some he evoked the horrors of society with ruthless realism (see 'Dances of Death'). Occasionally, too, he recorded moments of happiness (see 'The Impulses of Youth'), but the dominant note was one of desolation or even terror (see 'A Voice from the Chorus', 'Worlds Fly Past', and 'The Commander's Footsteps'). Blok called his world the 'terrible world'.

Nevertheless, hope did not entirely desert him; he knew that the Beautiful Lady still existed and looked forward to the day when the terrible world would be swept away by the Spirit of Music. His play *The Rose and the Cross* and many of his poems speak of the connection he saw between his suffering and the birth of a new joy (see 'Yes, this is the Call of Inspiration', 'Earth's Heart is Growing Cold again'. and 'I Want to Live'). In particular he was able to identify himself with poor suffering Russia (see 'Russia' and 'Autumn Day'); Russia also had lost the Beautiful Lady and was living through what he called the 'years of conflagration', but for her, too, a terrible release was in sight. He was all too acutely aware of the unpleasant aspects of his country, yet he knew that his fate was by now irrevocably bound up with hers (see 'Russia and I' and 'Shamelessly, Endlessly Sinning'). One of the most compelling sections of his third book is entitled *My Country*.

In 1911 Blok and his wife visited Brittany, where he gained ideas for *The Rose and the Cross* and for the poem 'Do You Remember'. In 1913 they returned to France for a holiday. Otherwise the years from 1909 to 1914 were not marked by any unusual events in his life; he continued to lead the life of the Petersburg intellectual, which in many ways he so much hated, and as before he spent summers at Shakhmatovo. In 1914, however, he surrendered himself once again to the elemental, as he had seven years before in his affair with Volokhova. This time he fell in love with the opera singer L.A. Delmas; he had seen her playing Carmen and dedicated to her a cycle of poems with the same name in which the gipsy music of desperate ecstasy finds its final expression – though now in a simpler, more classical form than in 1907 (see 'As the Ocean Changes Colour' and 'Among the Admirers of Carmen').

The outbreak of the war was for him the beginning of the purging storm which he had both feared and hoped for (see 'Those Born in the Years of Stagnation'). During the war he wrote very little poetry; 'The Kite' shows his reaction to Russia's sufferings at this time. In June 1916 he was called up and served uneventfully in the Pinsk marshes until March 1917. Meanwhile the February Revolution had come. Blok greeted it enthusiastically; on his return to Petrograd he wandered through the streets and shared the 'exceptional awareness that everything is possible . . . that a miracle has happened'. That summer he worked on the commission enquiring into the tsarist regime, whose findings he later published under the title *The Last Days of Imperial Power*. And as October approached he heard more and more clearly the roar of revolution and foresaw the cleansing fire. 'In Bolshevism', he wrote, 'there is a terrible truth'. His conception of revolution was above all musical; Marx and Lenin meant nothing to him, but he was on the side of the Bolsheviks, even though this meant breaking with many of his friends. It is this sort of belief in the Revolution which inspired 'The Twelve'.

This, his most famous poem, was written in a few days in January 1918. Writing it, he felt that, as with the actresses Volokhova in 1907 and Delmas in 1914, he was 'surrendering himself to the elemental'. On completing it, he wrote in his notebook: 'Today I am a genius.' Formally it is different from anything he had written before, but many of its themes are the themes which sound in his earlier writing. Through the poem blows the purging gale of the snowstorm, in which the old world, now represented by a few puppet-like figures and a mangy dog, is at last crumbling. The agents of its destruction are the twelve Red Guards, brutal, revengeful, yet childishly vulnerable. Their only good quality, if it is one, is their determination to march on through the blizzard and the night, disregarding purely personal tragedies (Kate's murder) which must be left behind with the rest of the old world. And yet these thugs, the 'scum of the earth', are seen at the end of the poem to be led by a force which transcends them. The twelve soldiers become the twelve apostles, led by the mysterious figure of Christ.

This figure has aroused a great deal of disapproval and controversy. Blok himself said he hated this 'feminine spectre', yet he always defended his poem, feeling that however unclearly he had expressed himself, Christ had to be there at the end. Who is this Christ then? It would clearly be surprising if he stood for historical Christianity or the Russian Orthodox Church, which Blok had repeatedly repudiated. But before the Christ of the Church, there was the Christ of the Gospels. Blok commented in his diary: '*If* there was a real clergy in Russia and not just a class of morally obtuse people of ecclesiastical calling, it would long ago have realized that "Christ is with the Red Guards". This is a truth that can hardly be denied, a simple matter for anyone who has read the Gospels and thought about them.' More generally, Christ seems to be akin to the Spirit of Music, which Blok saw as the motive force behind the Revolution; he is a sign that the cyclone of change is not purely destructive (like that of 'The Snow Mask'), but is directed to the long-awaited renovation of Russian society. Indeed, although one cannot simply identify this Christ with the Beautiful Lady, one is tempted to ask if there is not some connection between them. Blok never answered this question; in 1920, however, he wrote a note about the political significance of his poem:

I do not go back on what I wrote then, because it was written in harmony with the elemental: for instance, during and after the writing of 'The Twelve', for some days I physically felt and heard a great roar surrounding me, a continuous roar (probably the roar of the collapse of the old world). That is why those who see in 'The Twelve' a political poem are either blind to art or up to the ears in political filth or else in the grip of a great rage – whether they are friendly or hostile to my poem.

It would however be wrong to deny all connection between 'The Twelve' and politics. The truth is that the poem was written in that exceptional and always very brief period when the passing revolutionary cyclone raises a storm in every sea – nature, life and art; in the sea of human life there is a little backwater called politics . . . and in this glass of water at that time there was a storm – and how! – there was talk of abolishing diplomacy, creating a new justice and ending the war, which was already in its fourth year. The seas of nature, life and art were raging and the foam rose up in a rainbow over them. I was looking at that rainbow when I wrote 'The Twelve'; that is why some drops of politics remained in the poem.

Blok's last important poem, 'The Scythians', was written immediately after 'The Twelve'. Thereafter he wrote almost no poetry; his creative drive had abandoned him. Similarly, though it would be wrong to say that he rejected the October Revolution, he no longer felt towards it the enthusiasm he had felt in January 1918. The passage just quoted shows how fundamentally unpolitical a man he was; Trotsky said of him: 'Certainly Blok is not one of us, but he came towards us. And that is what broke him.' His last years were hard. In August 1921, after a long and painful illness, he died.

In two of the poems which we have translated, Blok speaks of his future readers. In 'To my Friends' he gloomily foresees the day when 'some latter-day academic' will reduce him to a 'definitive tome' and cries out in despair:

> Damn book, be silent!
> I never wrote you, never!

But in 'I Want to Live' he imagines a 'happier young man' of the future composing the epitaph he wanted:

> Forgive his moods – was the momentum
> bitterness that made him write?
> He was wholly on the side of freedom,
> he was wholly on the side of light!

A Red Glow in the Sky

A red glow in the sky, the dead night underground.
The pine trees imprison me in their dark destiny,
but unmistakeably there comes the sound
of a far distant, undiscovered city.

You will make out houses in heavy rows,
and towers, and the silhouette of buttresses,
and gardens behind stone walls sombre with shadows,
and arrogant ramparts of ancient fortresses.

Unmistakeably from submerged centuries
The piercing mind makes ready for dawning
the long forgotten roar of silted cities
and the rhythm of life returning.

10 June 1900

I Seek Salvation

I seek salvation.
My bonfires burn on the mountain summit –
they light the whole dark vault of blue.
But brighter than all is the gaze of my spirit
and You far off . . . but is it You?
I seek salvation.

Solemnly the choir of stars sings in the zenith.
I am reviled by every generation.
I have lit You a fire on the mountain summit,
but You are a vision.
I seek salvation.

The choir of stars grows weary and falls quiet.
Doubt disappears. The night is done.
There You descend from the far, bright summit.
Waiting for You, I have stretched out my spirit.
You bring salvation!

25 November 1900

The Intellect cannot Measure the Divine

The intellect cannot measure the divine,
azure is hidden from the intellect,
but seraphim sometimes bring as a sign
a holy vision to the world's elect.

I dreamt that I saw the Venus of Russia
wearing a heavy tunic once –
passionless her purity, joyless beyond measure,
a calm vision lighting her countenance.

Not for the first time she visited the world,
but for the first time there thronged her ways
different warriors, champions of a new mould . . .
and strange was the gleam in the depths of her eyes . . .

29 May 1901

I Sense Your Coming

> And the heavy sleep of worldly consciousness
> You will shake off, grieving and loving.
>
> *Vladimir Solovyov*

I sense Your coming. One year follows another.
Always in the same shape I sense Your coming.

The whole horizon is on fire – and mercilessly clear.
I wait in silence – *grieving and loving.*

The whole horizon is on fire for the apparition,
but terror pricks me: You will change Your shape.

Your coming will occasion insolent suspicion;
You will abandon Your familiar shape.

Oh, I shall fall, and fall with what bitterness,
my mortal dreams permitting no escape!

How clear the whole horizon is! Radiance approaches.
But terror pricks me: You will change Your shape.

4 June 1901

I Enter the Dark Church Slowly

I enter the dark church slowly
and perform a humble rite.
I wait for the Beautiful Lady
in the glimmer of icon light.

In shadow at a pillar's base
I tremble at the creak of the door;
with only an image lighting my face,
only a dream of Her.

How familiar the flowing gown
of her Eternal Majesty!
From lofty cornices float down
daydreams and smiles and fantasies.

How caressing the candles, Holy One,
how comforting Your brilliant head!
I hear no words, no sighing, none,
but I believe: Beloved.

25 October 1902

The Factory

Next door the windows are yellow.
As the night falls, as the night falls
the pensive bolt creaks and the people
come up to the gates in the wall.

The gates are shut holding them back,
but on the wall, but on the wall
someone motionless, someone black
is silently counting them all.

From this height I hear everything:
how with a brassy voice he barks
at those beneath him gathering
to bend their exhausted backs.

They will go in and set to work
shouldering sacks, while overhead
in yellow windows others will joke
about fleecing the common herd.

24 November 1903

Introduction to the Second Book of Poems

You have gone and will not be returning.
And hallowed be Your name!
Spears of the sunset once again burning
dip through the haze their shafts of flame.

To Your golden pipe one dark day
I shall set my lips wearily.
If my prayers have all drifted away,
oppressed, I shall sleep in the field.

You will pass in Your gold and purple –
and my eyes will no more be opened.
Let me rest in this somnolent world,
let me kiss the road's radiant end . . .

Tear my rusted soul out of my body!
Let me lie with the saints' holy band,
You, who preside over dry land and sea
with Your motionless slender hand!

April 1905

Illusion

Spring water thawed in an empty alley
gurgles as it goes, and a girl laughs lightly.
A drunken red dwarf will not let her pass.
Dancing, he kicks water over her dress.

She trembles, wraps herself round with a shawl.
Twilight edges in. The sun shifts round.
The dwarf jumps into the puddle like a ball,
raising ripples with a wrinkled hand.

The reflection frightens and attracts the girl.
A solitary street-lamp gives a distant wink.
The red sun has fallen behind the wall.
Laughter. Splashes. Drops of water. Factory stink.

Noises come faintly as if from a long way off . . .
Somewhere a dripping roof . . . somewhere an old man's cough . . .
Cold hands lifelessly cling to one another.
Eyes grow round, with no pupil in either.

How fearful! How deserted! In a fence's shadow
she lies a sodden bundle in the dark.
She weeps for the morning that must follow –
ashamed to return with the devil's mark . . .

Morning. Clouds. Smoke. Barrels upside down.
Blue sky dances where the bright ripples lift.
Red barriers are going up all over town.
Soldier boys come splashing past – left, right, left!

Down the alley by the damp fence in the dark,
his head shaking over the girl in her dream,
the monstrous dwarf is busily at work:
he drops two shoes – left, right – into the stream.

The shoes, turning round, ride off on the current,
and now a red cap overtakes them fast . . .
Laughter. Splashes. Drops of water. In a moment –
dog ears, beard, and a red frock coat come floating past . . .

They vanish – and ripples whisper indistinctly.
Imperceptibly the girl is waking:
red and blue spots caper in her vision.
Sequins of sunlight. Ripples. Splashes. Spring.

5 March 1904

The Little Priest of the Fen

On a thawed-out patch of green
in spring the little fen priest can be seen
at his vespers on his knees.

Over a tussock
his old black cassock
is a speck one hardly sees.

In the calm as the bleeding sun settles
you can see no turbulent devils,
but the magical twilight
has woven a spell over him with delicate hands . . .
little sounds as the sun descends,
rustle of night.

His prayers make no sound
and he smiles, and bows to the ground,
and he lifts his hat.

And he binds the damaged leg
of the lame and limping frog
with a grass's healing knot.
Then crossing him he sends him back:
'Off you go down your muddy track.
My soul is thankful
for every animal
for every breed
of beast, and every creed.'

And quietly he prays –
one hand on his hat-brim –
for the reed that sways,
for the frog's damaged limb,
for the Pope of Rome.

Fear not the bog-hole underfoot.
The little black cassock will pull you out.

17 April 1905

Autumn Freedom

I come out on the open highway
where the wind bends the springy bushes,
broken stone litters the verges,
barren strata of bright yellow clay.

In the damp valleys Autumn rampages
and has stripped the country graveyards bare,
but rowans in the roadside villages
can be seen shining scarlet from here.

There it is, my happiness, dancing
and ringing, lost in the undergrowth!
And far off, far off, beckoning
your embroidered sleeve's flowery cloth.

Who was it lured me out onto my road,
who was it laughed through my prison bars?
Or am I led on by the stony road,
a beggar, a singer of psalms?

No, I go out on the road under pressure
from no one. Earth, let your load be light!
I shall hear the voice of drunken Russia
and stretch out in a bar-room for the night.

I shall sing of good fortune, perhaps,
how my youth was dissolved in a glass . . .
or shall lose my heart to your open steppes,
and share the grief of your meadow grass . . .

There are many – free, young, and noble ones –
who will die not knowing love . . .
Shelter us in your boundless horizons!
Without you, how can we weep and live?

July 1905

A Girl was Singing

A girl was singing in the choir with fervour
of all who have known exile and distress,
of all the vessels that have left the harbour,
of all who have forgotten happiness.

Her voice soared up to the dome. Glistening,
a sunbeam brushed her shoulder in its flight,
and from the darkness all were listening
to the white dress singing in the beam of light.

It seemed to everyone that happiness
would come back, that the vessels all were safe,
that those who had known exile and distress
had rediscovered a radiant life.

The voice was beautiful, the sunbeam slender,
but up by the holy gates, under the dome,
a boy at communion wept to remember
that none of them would ever come home.

August 1905

The Stranger

These evenings over the restaurants
the air is hot and strangely cloying,
and shouts drift from the drunkards' haunts
on the putrid breath of spring.

Far off, over dusty side-streets can be seen –
over snug villas mile on mile –
the golden glint of a baker's sign,
and one can hear the children wail.

And every evening, past the level-
crossing, the jocular swells,
bowlers tilted at a rakish angle,
stroll between ditches with their girls.

Over the lake the rowlocks scraping
and women screeching can be heard,
and in a sky inured to everything
the moon leers down like a drunkard.

Each evening my one and only friend,
reflected at my glass's brink,
like me is fuddled and constrained
by the thick, mysterious drink.

And next to us, at the tables beside
our table, somnolent waiters pass
and drunks to one another, rabbit-eyed,
call out 'In vino veritas.'

Each evening, at the appointed moment
(or is this only in a dream?)
a girl's shape in a silken garment
shows dark against the window's steam.

And slowly between the drunkards weaving,
as always unescorted, there
she sits down by the window, leaving
a mist of perfume on the air.

And a breath of ancient legends gathers
about her silk dress as it swings,
about her hat with its mourning feathers,
and her slender hand with its rings.

And rooted there by this curious presence,
I search the shadowy veil once more
and through it see an enchanted distance
beyond an enchanted shore.

Vague confidences in my ear are loosed,
and the sun is suddenly mine,
and every crevice of my soul is sluiced
and flooded by the sticky wine.

And now the nodding ostrich-feather plume
begins to hypnotize my brain,
and eyes that are unfathomable bloom
blue on a distant shore again.

Deep in my soul there lies a treasure;
the only key to it is mine!
And you are right, you drunken monster!
I know now: there is truth in wine.

24 April 1906

Russia

Even sleeping you astonish me.
Russia, I cannot touch your gown.
I sleep, and in the mystery
behind my sleep you slumber on.

Russia, girdled with rivers
and your forests' intricate maze,
your cranes and your marshy acres,
and the sorcerer's cloudy gaze;

where peoples with differing features
from region to region, high and low,
at nightfall dance their choral dances
by their burning villages' glow;

where fortune-tellers and wizards
cast spells on the standing wheat,
and witches revel through blizzards
with demons in the whirling street;

where boisterous snowstorms cover
the poor hut to its pointed roof
and waiting for her faithless lover
a girl inside sharpens a knife;

where sapling shoots and branches flail
the crossroads and the country ways
and, whistling through bare twigs, the gale
sings legends of departed days . . .

Thus, in my dream, I have been shown
my country's terrible distress
and in the tatters of her gown
my soul conceals its nakedness.

I have taken the sorrowful lane
that leads to the churchyard gate
and there, stretched out on a tombstone,
have sung long songs all night –

not knowing to whom they were written,
or in what god I believed
with passionate conviction,
or who was the girl I loved.

Russia, your distances have rocked
a living soul to sleep, and see,
your cradling has not marked
its pristine purity.

I sleep, and in the mystery
behind my sleep she slumbers on.
Even sleeping she amazes me.
I cannot touch her gown.

24 September 1906

Snow Wine

Again, from the goblet, your presence
sparkling fills my heart with fear –
you with your smiling innocence
and your serpentine waves of hair.

Swept off my feet in the dark stream,
not loving, I again live through
a passionate forgotten dream
of kisses, of snowstorms masking you.

You laugh your magical laughter
and in the golden goblet sway,
and lightly over your sable fur
the currents of the blue wind play.

And how, looking into the liquor,
could I miss my Bacchic wreath?
and fail to remember your kisses,
my face upturned to meet your mouth?

29 December 1906

The blizzard sang.
And the snow flew in stinging swarms.
And my spirit was icebound.
You caught me in your arms.

Looking up, you threw your head back
and 'Look over there', you said, 'Look
Over there until you have
forgotten what you love.'

And you pointed to the lines of the city below,
to the sapphire acres under snow,
to the senseless cold.

And the snow's suspended hammer-stroke hurled
us into the gulf, where sparks scattered downwind
when snowflakes whirled uncertainly . . .

Sparks of a kind,
the hesitant snowflakes in their descent.
Rapidly, rapidly
above me you
overturned the blue
firmament . . .

The blizzard whirled up,
we saw a star drop
and then another . . .
and star after star
falling,
opening
abysses
to the windswept galaxies.

The sky held dark eyes that shed their light
brilliantly from it.
And I forgot the shapes
of the beautiful landscapes
in your radiance, comet!
In your radiance, snow-silvered night!

And past us, trailing their wreckage,
rushed the exorbitant years,
as if the heart in its ice-age
had sunk and would not reappear.

But beyond the far Pole wanders
my heart's sun haphazardly
in the grip of the icy nimbus
of your wild anarchy.

So rise in the frost, exorbitant blaze
of morning! Over the far
blue levels of distance raise
the standard of the fallen tsar.

3 January 1907

O Spring without End

O Spring without end, without limit –
endless and limitless dream!
I recognize you and salute
you, Life, with the clang of my shield!

I welcome you, failure, and after,
my greetings, success – here's
my hand. Nothing is shameful in laughter
or the spellbound valley of tears.

Argumentative midnights I welcome,
dark curtains that pale as they swing,
inflamed eyes renewed by the rhythm,
the intoxication of spring.

I welcome remote country villages
and the wells rising under the towns,
the firmament's star-studded spaces
and the slaves' bitter sweat in the mines.

At the threshold I meet you today –
as the wind through your snaking hair whips –
with a god's secret name locked away
in your cold and implacable lips.

In the face of this hostile encounter
you will never see my shield fall . . .
nor I your uncovered shoulders . . .
but a wild dream is over us all!

I look and I measure your venom
with my own hatred, curses, and love:
your torments, your ruin – I know them –
no matter: I welcome you, Life!

24 October 1907

42

O *What is the Setting Sun's Radiance to Me*

O what is the setting sun's radiance
to me, or broken hearts left behind,
when all I can see is a whirling dance
and trembling hands intertwined.

I catch sight of an ivory face
and swanlike I see her move;
I can hear the spirited voice.
O delicate name that I love!

And new dreams hurtling over me
trouble me on my rough road . . .
The falling snow still cannot cover me
in folds of its thickening shroud . . .

Fly, whirl, inflict me with torments,
snowflakes – wild glacial portents . . .
gossamer tendrils that bind
my soul, break loose, burn, and unwind . . .

You, my cold one, colder than ice,
something passionate stirs in my mind . . .
Heart, disconsolate hermit, rise;
and stifle your hymns, let them die . . .

Once more it's flying, flying,
once more it rings, and flakes whirl, advance –
a shower of snow-blind
sparks sweeps downwind . . .

You, like a vision, in a dance
with your companions move
round and round on a great expanse
of snow, a rapid
overlapping curve . . .

I can hear your spirited voice,
I catch sight of your ivory face,
bright eyes return my gaze . . .

All that I cannot phrase
a smile will have to convey . . .
Happiness! Night is with us!
But again, on your tremulous

course, you veer away . . .
And the snow in a whirling cloud,
beginning to raise
a song, has caught up and shrouded
your slim
and supple limbs.

And the blizzard, the blizzard, once
again sings, whirls, whines . . .
Here betrayal, there illusion . . .

In the snowy goblet shines
intoxication . . .
resonance . . .
Swirl and swerve,
(heart, be silent), weave

snowflakes where her feet have been –
Death is put down!
In the dark meadow
light moves to and fro!
Years of misfortune
I have seen . . .

And look – she has set off again,
dancing the other way . . .
The blizzard sings. Your voice is plain.
Swiftly you sway
into the dance – who lit
my mortal eyes
for one split second . . .

What does the light mean, and what is the dance
with which you lure and beckon?
When will the violence
of your dancing slacken?
What music? And who sings?
What have I to fear?
Sad music from sad strings
and – limitless Russia?

And as in a nightmare's hideous maelstrom,
the sky is split open, earth shrinks underneath,
and there, as in torment, as in delirium,
are daring, confusion, oblivion, death –
You gather momentum!
Your arms are flung
forward . . . the song
sweeps on . . .
And a strange glow suffuses your countenance . . .
That daring dance!
O song! O daring! O mask! O ruin!
Accordeon!

1 November 1907

Accordeon

Accordeon, accordeon!
Squeal and blaze up! Hey, sing!
Hey, little yellow buttercups,
flowers of the spring!

With a whirling and a whistling,
carousing till daybreak.
The bushes, gently rustling,
motion to me – 'Look.'

Look – arms uplifted she has spun
into a dance, has flung
her flowers over everyone,
and melted into song . . .

Capricious, cunning woman,
dance! Deceiving girl,
forever and ever poison
my godforsaken soul!

I shall go crazy and berserk,
raving that I love you,
that you are all the night, all dark,
that I am drunk on you . . .

that you have robbed me of my soul –
the soul you poisoned –
that I sing of you, you, girl,
songs without end.

9 November 1907

She Came in from the Frost

She came in from the frost
with her cheeks glowing,
and she filled the room
with a scent of air and perfume,
with her voice ringing
and her utterly work-shattering
chatter.

Immediately she dropped on the carpet
the fat slab of an art magazine
and suddenly it seemed
that in my generous room
was a shortage of space.

This was all a little annoying
not to say silly.
What's more, all at once she wanted
me to read *Macbeth* to her.

Hardly had we got to the 'earth's bubbles',
of which I cannot speak without emotion,
when I noticed that she too was moved
and was staring out of the window.

And there was a big tabby cat
inching its way down the gable
in pursuit of some passionate pigeons.

I was annoyed most of all because
it was not us but the pigeons who were kissing
and that the times of Paolo and Francesca were over.

6 February 1908

On the Field of Kulikovo

I

The river opens out, crawls grieving on its way
washing its banks; a steep
embankment of barren yellow clay;
stooks grieve in the steppe.

Russia, my darling Russia, painfully
clear is the road we ride!
Like the arrow of Tartar liberty
road pierces side.

Our road lies over the steppe and through infinite
anguish, your anguish, Russia:
even the night beyond the frontier limit
I do not fear.

Let the night come. Until our camp-fires star
the steppe we gallop.
The Khan's bright sabre and the holy banner
flash in the smoke of the steppe . . .

Endless the battle! Blood and dust cover
our dream of peace.
The wild mare of the steppe sweeps on, on, over
the feather-grass . . .

endlessly! Milestone and precipice flicker . . .
draw rein!
The clouds in terror huddle closer, thicker,
sunset's a bloodstain!

Sunset's a bloodstain! The heart's blood dropping!
Weep, heart, weep . . .
There is no rest. The wild mare galloping
knows no sleep.

II

At midnight there we halted together,
beyond the point of no return.
The swans across the Nepryadva
were calling, calling, swan after swan . . .

On the road is a white stone burning,
beyond the river the pagan horde.
The banner over our returning
troops will never again tug at its cord.

Head bowed, eyes on the ground, my friend utters
these words: 'Sharpen your sword for the wars
still to be fought against the Tartars:
offer your life for the holy cause.'

I am not the first, nor the last, warrior.
Many years more will my country suffer.
Remember then at your morning prayer
one who loved you, my darling Russia.

III

When Mamai's cavalry ringed in darkness
steppes and bridges, on the grey
field of battle, lady, You were with us –
and yet were far away.

In the middle of the plain at nightfall,
by the sombre Don,
I heard Your voice in my prophet's heart call
with the cry of the swan.

From midnight gathering, as clouds gather,
the Prince's men moved up,
and far, far away a sobbing mother
clung to a stirrup.

While the night birds, circling, circling,
sailed in the distance,
silent over Russia summer lightning
championed the Prince.

Threatening carnage to the Tartar host
all night the eagles cried.
The Nepryadva veiled herself in mist
like a royal bride.

And You came down in a radiant dress,
over the misted
river rocking in its sleep. My horse
never turned its head.

Like a wave of silver through the darkness
pouring from my blade
You came, lightening the dusty harness
that on my shoulders weighed.

And when, next morning, the horde moved on
darkening the field,
made by no human hands Your image shone
permanent in my shield.

IV

Again with the grief of centuries
feather-grass is bowed to the ground.
Beyond the misted river's mysteries
you call me with a faint far sound.

Untraceable on the horizon
the herds of wild horses are lost.
Under the sway of a waning moon
a new ferocity is loosed.

Grief-stricken, wandering like a wolf
under a white moon on the wane,
I don't know what to do with myself
or where I shall find you again.

I listen to weapon on weapon
hammering and the trumpet's cry.
Out of earshot a conflagration
gnaws, red-toothed, at the Russian sky.

Obsessed with prophecy, I wander
sick at heart on a horse as white
as the unreined clouds I encounter
riding high in the misty night.

Radiant visions leap up, leap up –
exhalations from a wounded
heart – and radiant visions drop
burnt by a dark fire in my head.

'Come down, my marvellous marvel!
Teach me to shine like you.' The wind
is lifting my horse's mane. Rival
swords clash in the wake of the wind.

V

The mist of inescapable disasters
veiled the face of the coming day.
Vladimir Solovyov

Over the field of Kulikovo
again the mist rose, spread, and lay
draped like a fallen cloud to cover
the face of the coming day.

Behind the unscarred silence, under
the infiltrating mist
you cannot hear the battle thunder
nor see the battle lightning twist.

But I perceive you now, beginning
of high turbulent days. Once more
over the enemy camp the winging
of swans is heard, swans trumpeting War.

51

The heart cannot live peaceably.
Now not for nothing does the air
darken, armour hang heavily.
Your hour has struck. To prayer!

June–December 1908

To my Friends

Damned strings, be silent!
Maikov

We secretly hate one another,
are envious, deaf, and estranged,
but how can one labour and live without
hatred too old to be changed?

So what? When every one of us
has poisoned his house with hatred;
the walls are all sodden with venom,
and there's nowhere to lay one's head!

So what? Having lost faith in happiness
we laugh till we foam at the lips
and drunkenly watch from the pavement
our houses cave in and collapse!

We are traitors in life and friendship,
we are spinners of empty words.
So what? We are clearing the way
for those who come afterwards.

When under a fence in the nettles
our wretched bones sift back to loam,
some latter-day academic
will write a definitive tome . . .

and, damn him, no doubt he will torture
innocent lads with textual notes,
with births and deaths linked by a hyphen,
and a jumble of haphazard quotes . . .

How sad that our lives are so tangled,
so painful and so frenetic,
and shall be the preserve of a pedant
and beget a fresh litter of critics . . .

Oh, for that grave in the nettles
in which to sleep and forever
forget oneself! Damned books, be silent;
I never wrote you, never!

24 July 1908

Russia

Again, as in the golden age,
three breech-straps flogging at the trot
and the painted spokes of the carriage
bog down in a muddy rut.

Russia, my beggarly Russia,
your grey huts in their clusters,
your songs set to the wind's measure
touch me like love's first tears.

I cannot offer you my pity,
I carry my cross as I can . . .
Squander your wild beauty
on every new magician!

If they seduce you and deceive you,
you'll not be broken or collapse;
though suffering may overshadow
the beauty of your face perhaps . . .

but what of that? Just one more sorrow,
one more tear added to the Don,
and you unaltered – forests, meadows,
and the patterned scarf pulled well down . . .

And the impossible is possible,
the highroad is light and long,
and the glint of an eye far off
glances from under the scarf
as prison-weary, sorrowful,
begins the troika-driver's song.

18 October 1908

I am Nailed to a Bar with Liquor

I am nailed to a bar with liquor.
Been drunk all day. So what! I've lost
my happiness – gone in a troika
careering into silver mist.

It flies on a troika, vanishing
in centuries, the snow of time . . .
Only the soul is drowning, sinking
under the horseshoes' silver stream.

Their sparks into the darkness flutter;
all night, all night the sparks blaze on . . .
and bells on the shaft-bow mutter
that happiness has come and gone.

And only the golden harness
can be seen all night, heard all night . . .
and you, soul . . . deaf soul . . . are hopeless-
ly drunk, dead drunk, hopelessly tight.

26 October 1908

Chivalry

Chivalry, honour, exploits, fame
I had forgotten on this bitter earth
while your face circled by a simple frame
shone before me on the tablecloth.

The hour came, you left the house for ever.
I hurled the ring after you into the dark.
You laid your life in the hands of another
and I forgot your cheekbone's lovely arc.

The days flew by, a cursed swarm and unending,
while love-affairs and liquor soured my mouth . . .
Remembering you at the altar standing,
I called for you again, as for my youth . . .

I called for you, but you didn't acknowledge me,
I wept for you, but you didn't come down.
You wrapped yourself round in a blue cloak sadly
and went into the wet night on your own.

I do not know where your pride found a pillow,
my dear one, my tender one, my delight.
In all my dreams I see the blue cloak billow
at your back, departing into the night.

No dreaming now of tenderness, of fame;
everything has gone, vanished with my youth.
I have taken your face in its simple frame
with a stroke of my hand from the tablecloth.

30 December 1908

Autumn Day

Not hurrying, my quiet friend
and I walk through the stubble,
and my soul is unburdened
as in a village chapel.

The autumn day is still and clear,
a crow raucously scoffing
at others is all you can hear,
and an old woman coughing.

Mist spreads beside the barn like gauze,
and long there under cover
we follow with a steady gaze
the cranes streaming over . . .

They fly, in a sharp wedge they fly;
the leader cries out, keening . . .
Why does he cry out, why, why?
This grief – what is its meaning?

And the down-at-heel villages
no eye can count or measure . . .
and burning a hole in the dusk
a fire in a distant pasture . . .

Poor land, poor land, what do you mean
to the heart that moves in me?
Poor love, poor love, poor wife of mine,
why do you weep so bitterly?

1 January 1909

They do not Trade, Sleep or Remember

They do not trade, sleep, or remember.
The bells of Easter, groan on groan,
tearing the thick night with their thunder,
ring out over the pitch-black town.

Over all of man's creation
hammered by him into the earth,
over death, pain, and degradation
they ring the bells for all they're worth . . .

Over the world's mess they ring out;
over all wrongs that can't be put right;
they ring out over the fur coat
which you were wearing on that night.

30 March 1909

Ravenna

All that passes, all that perishes
your centuries have buried. Held
in the arms of somnolent ages
you sleep, Ravenna, like a child.

Slaves no longer through the Roman gate
bring the bright mosaic colours.
And the gilt is burning out
on walls of cool basilicas.

The rough-hewn crypts, imperceptibly
softening in the damp's embraces,
hold the green sarcophagi
of holy monks and empresses.

The burial vaults were never stiller,
their steps are cold, curtained with gloom,
lest the eyes of the blessed Galla
opening should burn her tomb.

The battle clangour is forgotten,
battle scars, battle stains effaced,
lest the voice of Placidia, risen,
should sing of passion from the past.

The sea has marched back, roses grapple
the fortress wall, lest in his grave
Theodoric sleeping under marble
should dream of turbulence above.

Sepulchral wastes where the grapes fatten,
tomblike the people, houses, rooms.
Only the bronze of solemn latin
sings like a trumpet from the tombs.

Only at times, in the calm and steady
eyes of Ravenna girls I discern
a sadness passing shyly
for a sea that will not return.

Only at nights, over the meadows,
over the accounts of the years
to come, Dante's aquiline shadow
sings of the New Life at my ear.

May–June 1909

Florence

I

Die, Florence, Judas, disappear
in the twilight of long ago!
In the hour of love and in the hour
of death I'll not remember you.

Oh, laugh at yourself today, Bella,
for your features have fallen in.
Death's rotten wrinkles disfigure
that once miraculous skin.

The motorcars snort in your lanes,
your houses fill me with disgust;
you have given yourself to the stains
of Europe's bilious yellow dust.

The bicycles ring in the dust
where Savonarola faced the flame,
where Leonardo knew the dusk,
and where Beato's blue dream came.

Your sumptuous Medicis shudder,
your trampled lilies you deface,
but your own life you cannot recover
in the dust of the marketplace!

The slow groan of the Mass, the charnel
stink of roses in the nave –
may all that cumbersome ritual
melt in time's scouring wave!

II

You, Florence, are a tender iris.
For whom did I hunger and thirst
all day, with a love deep and hopeless,
in your Cascine gardens' dust?

How good to remember hopelessness,
to dream in your seclusion, stroll
in ancient heat and in the tenderness
of my no longer stripling soul . . .

But we are divorced by destiny,
and over far lands to the south
your smoky iris will return to me
in dreams like the days of my youth.

III

In a long and serene embrace
my soul is tightly bound,
the smoky iris, tender iris
breathing its fragrance round
commands me to cross rivers
on wings as the wind flies,
commands me to drown forever
deep in those twilit skies,
and when I surrender myself
to the last heat of the day,
blue heat, a blue wave in a gulf
of blue, will carry me away . . .

IV

Sunbeaten, burning stone scorches
my fever-misted sight.
Under the flame smoky irises
seem poised as if for flight.

O, inconsolable misery!
I know you by heart, despair!
Into the black sky of Italy
with a black soul I stare.

V

False windows on a black sky opening,
and a spotlight picking out a palace.
There she goes, in her patterned clothing
with a smile on her swarthy face.

And wine already troubles my sight
and its fire has entered my bloodstream . . .
Signora, what shall I sing you tonight,
what shall I sing to sweeten your dream?

VI

Beneath the listless heat of Florence
your heart is emptier; carpeted
in silence are the steps of the churches;
and every flower hangs its head.

Keep a watch on the dregs of your heart
and have the artist's lie in mind:
for only in the skiff of art
can you leave the dreary world behind.

VII

In a blue smoke haze
rises the evening heat,
ruler of Tuscany . . .

On and on it sways
under lamps in the street
like a bat in no hurry . . .

Already in the valleys
lights without number glow,
and from the jeweller's window
gleam answering galaxies,
and mountains have eclipsed
the town with blue twilight;
with street songs on their lips
signore welcome the night.

The iris smokes in the dust,
in the Lacryma Christi
a light foam rises . . .

Dance and sing at the feast,
Florence, you deceiver,
in a wreath of scorched roses . . .

Incite my blood to madness
with passionate songs,
and make the night sleepless
and break the strings
and beat your tambourine,
to drown the sobs that rise
out of an empty lane
where your soul cries . . .

May–August 1909

Russia and I

Russia and I, must we suffer one destiny?
Tsar and Siberia, Yermak and gaol!
Oh, for a change of direction, heart, company . . .
what has your gloom to attract a free soul!

When did you ever know anything? When did you
trust in God? What have your ballads to say?
The Chud conjured up and the Merya mapped for you
forest tracks, roads, milestones showing the way.

Down by your rivers you hewed hulls and settlements,
but holy Byzantium you never saw . . .
Hawks and wild swans you let loose on your distances
and from the steppes watched a black mist pour.

Over the Black Sea and over the White, and on
into black nights and into white days
wildly a rigid face stares from the dark unknown,
Tartar eyes into the dark unknown blaze . . .

Ember-red over your camp every evening
there is a silent, continual glow . . .
Flickering dream-mirage, why are you signalling?
Why do you toy with my free soul so?

28 February 1910

Hard to be Moving among Them

'A man has burnt out there'

Fet

Hard to be moving among them
pretending to be still alive,
proclaiming the heart's delirium
to those who have still to live.

And in your nightmare hard to find
a pattern to its maelstrom rage,
that by the flickering of your page
they know the holocaust behind.

10 May 1910

A Voice from the Chorus

How often we sit weeping – you
and I – over the life we lead!
My friends, if you only knew
the darkness of the days ahead!

Today you press your darling's hand,
lightheartedly you fondle it;
only to weep for a lie behind
her lips, or a knife in her hand –
poor child, poor child!

Lies have no ending, nor deceit.
Death keeps its distance.
The dark world will grow darker yet,
wilder the whirl of the planets
for centuries hence.

And we shall see the apocalypse,
the last, worst age descend.
Repulsive evil will eclipse
the sky, laughter freeze on all lips,
a longing for life's end . . .

You will be waiting, child, for spring –
and spring will fool you.
You will call for the sun's rising –
the sun will lie low.
And your shout, when you start shouting,
silence will swallow . . .

So, quieter than water now,
lower than grass, be contented
with your lives. Children, if you knew
the darkness of the days ahead!

6 June 1910

The Commander's Footsteps

At the door hangs a heavy curtain
like the night mist at the pane.
What of your freedom now, Don Juan,
never to be free from fear again?

Cold and empty is the sumptuous bedroom,
servants sleep in the quilting dark.
From a faraway blessed kingdom
comes the rough call of a cock.

What to a traitor are sounds of the blessed?
Life ebbs in a dwindling stream.
Donna Anna sleeps, hands crosswise on her breast,
Donna Anna dreams a dream.

Whose the cruel features, whose the iron
face that in the mirror gleams?
Anna, is the grave so sweet to lie in,
sweet to dream unearthly dreams?

Life is frenzied, fathomless, empty!
Fate, old Fate, come out and fight!
Passionate, triumphant, in reply
through the mist a horn sings out.

Owl-eyed, splashing the night with its lamps,
silently a car swoops past.
Muffled footsteps: the Commander tramps
heavily into the house at last . . .

Open door. Out of the cold comes up a
sound like midnight striking, striking near,
hoarsely striking. 'You asked me to supper.
Are you ready? I am here.'

To the cruel question comes no answer.
Silence. In the sumptuous bedroom
daybreak lifts the latch to terror.
Servants sleep in the blanching gloom.

At the hour of daybreak it grows colder;
at the hour of daybreak a dark sky.
Lady of light! Where are you, Donna Anna?
Anna! Anna! No reply.

Only the mist-muffled clock replies –
striking for the last time – with
At your death Donna Anna will rise,
Anna will rise at your hour of death.

September 1910

From *Retribution*
Book 2

I

In those far years of inertia
sleep misted men's imaginings:
Pobedonostsev over Russia
extended owl-like wings,
and there was no sunset or sunrise
but the wings' wide shadow alone;
a magic circle he had thrown
round Russia, fathoming her eyes
with a wizard's glassy stare.
It is not difficult to spell-
bind beauty with a marvellous tale
and soon she could not stir –
her hopes, thoughts, passions put to sleep . . .
but even subdued by black magic
a healthy glow coloured her cheek;
and in the magician's grip
she seemed abundantly strong,
but with her strength compressed
and useless in an iron fist . . .
The wizard with one hand swung
a censer, from which in flight
a smoking stream of incense leaped . . .
but with the other hand he swept
living souls out of sight.

II

In those unmemorable years
St Petersburg was even grimmer,
although, where the fortress rears,
the moving water was no greyer
in the measureless river . . .
A bayonet gleamed, bells grieved, the same

71

young flappers and fops as ever
careering to the Islands came,
and a horse with the same soft laugh
answered a horse on the home trip,
and – snagged with furs – a black moustache
tickled eyelashes and lips . . .
To think how once I would career
along with you, oblivious
to all the world! But it's no use
and not much happiness, my dear.

III

In those years the terrible dawn
had scarcely showed red in the East . . .
The Petersburg mob was drawn
to gawp at the tsar like a beast . . .
The surging people shuffled their feet,
a coachman brilliant with the gleam
of medals whipped up his team,
a policeman in the street
was keeping the crowd orderly . . .
A loud voice bellows 'Hurrah!'
and, huge and blubbery, the tsar
drives past with all his family.
It's spring, but the sun shines dully,
with Easter still seven weeks off,
and a freezing drip from the roof
already creeps under my collar
and down, making my teeth chatter . . .
Wherever you turn, the wind's a knife
at your ribs . . . 'It's a terrible life' –
avoiding a puddle – you mutter;
a dog gets under your feet,
light glints on a spy's galoshes,
an acid smell blows from each back-street,
and the rag-and-bone man shouts 'Old dresses!'

And meeting a stranger's stare,
you would like to spit in his face
if only you didn't notice
the very same wish there.

IV

But before the nights of midsummer
when all the city would lie
asleep under an outstretched sky,
a great moon over your shoulder
grew red mysteriously
before the measureless dawn . . .
O, my elusive city,
why from the chasm were you born? . . .
Remember: coming one white night
to where the sphinx stares out to sea,
and leaning on the rough-hewn granite
with head bowed, distantly,
distantly, you could hear
an ominous seaward sound,
impossible for God's atmosphere
and improbable on land . . .
You saw with the eye of the angel
high on the fortress spire; and there –
(dream or reality) a fair
fleet blocking the Neva channel
suddenly from shore to shore . . .
The Mighty Founder, Peter the Great,
himself stood on the first frigate . . .
This was a dream that many saw . . .
What dreams and what storms, Russia,
await you in the coming times?

But in those days of inertia
not everyone, of course, dreamed dreams . . .
and then there was nobody there
when the moment of vision came.
(One lover, out late in the square
with upturned collar, hurried home . . .)

But, crimson-streaked, behind the ships
the day was already dawning,
and already the pennant tips
were waking to the wind of morning,
and the measureless dawn already
was pointing a bloody finger
towards Tsushima and Port-Arthur,
towards the ninth of January . . .

March 1911

Yes. This is the call of inspiration.
My daydreams constantly revert
to places of humiliation,
darkness, poverty, and dirt . . .
Down there, down there, humbler, lower,
the other world can better be seen . . .
Have you seen the kids in Paris cower,
or the tramps by the wintry Seine?
Open your eyes to all the blind
horror of life, open them fast,
before the great storm's sudden blast
strips the face of your native land –
let righteous anger ripen in you,
prepare your hands for the work to come . . .
or if you cannot – then let boredom
and grief gather and burn in you . . .
but, without more ado, wipe off
the greasepaint mask of this sham life,
and like the timid mole dig down
from light into the earth – lie prone
and still, hating life fiercely,
despising all the world and – though
you cannot see the future clearly –
saying to the present: NO.

September 1911

Earth's Heart is Growing Cold again

Earth's heart is growing cold again.
I meet the cold with my head up.
For mankind in the desert I maintain
an undivided love.

Behind this love anger and scorn rise
and ripen. I long to see written
in men's eyes and in women's eyes
marks of damnation and election.

'Poet,' they'll cry, 'forget, have done.
To the beautiful refuges return.'
No! Better in this cold to burn!
There is no refuge, no peace, none.

1911

Do You Remember

Do you remember – the green water
sleeping in the arms of our bay
and how, in line ahead, the warships
sailed in from the sea that day?

Four of them – grey ones. And questions
excited us for one whole hour,
and sailors tanned by exotic suns
swaggered past us on the pier.

The world widened, put on mystery.
Then suddenly the ships sailed out.
And we could see the four hulls bury
themselves in the ocean and the night.

The ocean was simply the ocean
again. The lighthouse flashed away
glumly when the semaphore station
had signalled goodbye to the day.

How little we need to our lives' end,
we children – you and I,
for the heart is glad to be gladdened
by the merest novelty.

Discover by chance on the hinge
of a pocket knife some foreign dust –
and the world will again seem strange,
enveloped in a rainbow mist.

1911

Dances of Death

I

How hard for a dead man to pretend to be
alive and lusty among living ones!
But he must worm his way into society
hiding, for his job's sake, the rattle of bones.

The living sleep. The dead man climbs from his coffin,
and goes to the House, to the bank, the bar . . .
The paler the night, the blacker his chagrin,
and pens scratch triumphantly hour by hour.

All day the dead man drafts a memorandum.
The office doors are closing. Watch him, hear
him whispering – wagging his bottom –
whispering smut in a Deputy's ear.

Evening draws on, with rain and soot splashing
the passers-by, houses, and all that trash . . .
To other filth the dead man is dashing
in a taxi-cab with a creaking spring.

The dead man hurries to a ballroom full
of people and pillars. He is wearing tails.
His hostess, a fool, and her husband, a fool,
receive him at the door with gracious smiles.

He is tired by a day at the office slaving,
but the rattle of bones is drowned by the band . . .
He must pretend to be one of the living!
Firmly he takes hold of a friendly hand –

Beside a pillar his eyes encounter
those of his partner – she, like him, is dead.
Behind their conventional party banter
you can hear the truth that remains unsaid:

'Exhausted friend, in this room I feel foreign.'
'Exhausted friend, the grave is cold as snow.'
'It's twelve already.' 'You haven't asked N.N.
to waltz with you, and she loves you so . . .'

And there is N.N., searching with a wild look
for him, for him. There's thunder in her blood
and in her face, beautiful but childlike,
the meaningless rapture of living love.

He whispers words that have no meaning,
enchantments that the living so desire,
and he observes how her head is leaning
on her shoulder, how her cheeks catch fire . . .

The old familiar and malicious poisons
he pours into her ear with more than malice.
'How much he loves me. How clever he is!'

She hears a strange unearthly clatter – his
castanet rattle of bones on bones.

19 February 1912

II

Night, street, a lamp, a chemist's window,
a senseless and dim light. No doubt
in a quarter century or so
there'll be no change. There's no way out.

You'll die, and just the same as ever
begin the dance again. A damp
night, frozen ripples on the river,
a chemist's shop, a street, a lamp.

10 October 1912

III

An empty street. One light in a window.
The jewish chemist groans to his pillow.

In front of a cupboard stencilled *Poison*,
hinging his creaking knees, a skeleton

wrapped to the eyes in a waterproof cloak
is searching for something, with a black joke

twisting his jaws. He has it, but his bones
knock something, his skull turns . . . the chemist moans,

half rises – and rolls over . . . Meanwhile
the visitor hands a precious phial

from under his cloak to a noseless pair
of women, outside in the streetlamp's stare.

October 1912

IV

An old, old dream. Down the night's tunnel
streetlamps striding – to what end?
Only black water beyond,
and then oblivion. Round

a street-corner sidles a shade;
another creeps to its side –
parted cloak, white breast displayed,
a red flower riding one lapel.

Is it a warrior in a suit
of armour, or a bride in lace?
Helmet and feathers. No face.
A case of *rigor mortis*.

A bell in the gate strikes up.
Latches lift, rattle and drop.
Over the threshold step
a playboy and a prostitute.

Frozen stiff the winds bellow.
Darkness empty and still.
Upstairs, light on a sill.
What the hell!

The water is black as lead;
oblivion in it. A third
phantom. Where do you wander,
slipping from shadow to shadow?

7 February 1914

V

Tycoons are on the up and up.
Tenants are trampled down.
Brilliant as a buttercup
the moon shines on the town.

And it sheds a quiet light
that underlines the height
of the sheer stone surfaces
and darkened cornices . . .

All this would be meaningless
were the tsar not over us
to see that laws are honoured.

But don't look for a palace
or a good-natured face
with a crown on its forehead.

Down from the steppe he tramps;
down an avenue of lamps
now he's appearing.

There's a rag around his throat.
Between cap's brim and coat
the face is leering.

7 February 1914

The Impulses of Youth

The impulses of youth, again –
vigour and vision bursting out . . .
but now no happiness – and none then.
That much at least is beyond doubt!

Come through the dangerous years alive.
They lie in wait, go where you will,
but if you meet them and survive
you will at last believe the miracle,

and in the long run it will seem
there was no need for happiness,
that this unreasonable dream
but lasted half your life, or less;

that the lip of the cup has spilled
creative ecstasy like wine,
and everything is ours – not mine –
and a bond has been forged with the world,

and you'll recall from time to time,
with a faint smile of tenderness,
that mirage, adolescent dream
they once called happiness!

19 June 1912

Worlds Fly Past

Worlds fly past. Years fly past. The empty
universe darkly looks down on us.
And you, my shuttered soul, deafened and weary,
keep on about happiness, happiness.

What's happiness? The cool hour of twilight
in a fading garden or a forest trail;
forbidden entertainment, the dark delights
of liquor, lust, and the soul's betrayal?

What's happiness? A moment free from trouble,
a little sleep, a brief oblivion . . .
You wake – the crazy, incomprehensible,
heart-lacerating flight snatches you on.

You sigh with relief, look, the danger's over . . .
but no sooner said than – jerked again –
the top sets off, spinning in another
direction, humming as if insane.

And clinging to the slippery sharp rim,
and hearing a drone that never ceases,
we go mad in the gaudy continuum
of causes and effects, times and spaces.

When will the end come? How can we stand
this merciless racket that jars the brain . . .
The world is terrible! Give me your hand,
brother, friend. Let's forget ourselves again.

2 July 1912

To the Muse

There is in your secret refrain
a foreboding of all you destroy,
a cursing of sacred commandments
and a profanation of joy.

And such a magnetic attraction
that I can accept what they say:
that you brought down the angels from heaven,
that your beauty enticed them away . . .

And whenever you mock belief, suddenly
above you there shines in the air
that indistinct, purple-grey circle
which I have seen sometime, somewhere.

Are you evil or good? You are foreign,
and strange are the stories they tell
of you: muse and bright marvel for some,
but for me a monster from hell.

I cannot explain why, at daybreak,
with my strength ebbing out like a wave,
I did not go under but saw you
and asked for the comfort you gave.

I wanted us two to be enemies,
so why did you give me a field
full of flowers and a sky full of galaxies –
the curse that your beauty revealed?

Northern nights were never more treacherous,
golden wine never more potent,
gipsy love never more transient
than your terrible embrace . . .

And there was a dark exultation
in sacred things torn apart,
and, bitter as wormwood, this passion
was a wild delight to my heart.

29 December 1912

The Song of the Wind

It sings, it sings . . .
It sings and goes about the house . . .
And grief and tenderness and weariness
pluck as before at the heartstrings . . .

It is not onerous
the load of your life you carry along,
and with an endless simple song
time lulls and fondles us . . .

We are so old
and the world so
old,
and the lyre
sings of snow
in grey winter,
sings to us of grey winter's snow . . .

To lie there
on the snowy breast
of the last night . . .
to sigh, and shut
your eyes
forever,
to shut them in the night's embrace . . .

Passions and thoughts alike
return no more . . .
but look, look –
with a midnight roar
the wind of nightfall blows our way . . .
and the last light
is quenched. Die.
Quenched, the last light of the day.

19 October 1913

I, on your wedding days, funerals, holidays,
listen and wait under heatwave and blizzard
stifled with boredom I long to have swept away,
chased by a gentle note never yet heard.

There – it begins! And with cold concentration
I wait to capture it, leave it for dead,
while in advance of my keen expectation
stretches its barely discernible thread.

Is it a wind from the ocean, a heavenly
choir in the leaves? Has time stopped? Is it spring –
snow from the apple-trees scattering evenly?
Is it the pulse of an angel's wing?

Sound gathers, motion and daylight increase, as my
hours stretch out, carrying all that I know.
Yesterday wildly stares into tomorrow's eye.
There is no present, no pitiful 'now'.

And when at last the conception is imminent –
new soul, new forces about to draw breath –
meteor-like a curse strikes. In a moment
artifice chokes inspiration to death.

Then in a glacial cage I incarcerate
this gentle bird, this wind-following featherweight,
bird that intended to break death's control,
bird that descended to rescue my soul.

Here is my cage, an immovable metal one,
now with the sunset's brush gilding its grill.
Here is my bird, my once jubilant little one,
perched in a ring singing over my sill.

Those wings are clipped, all those songs learnt by heart. Are you
happy to stand sometimes under my sill?
So the songs please you. But waiting for something new,
stifled with boredom, I'm listening still.

12 December 1913

87

I Want to Live

I want to live, live to distraction:
to make the present live for ever,
make the impersonal human, cover
with flesh whatever now has none!

What if life's torpor stifles me,
what if I suffocate and am dumb –
a happier young man maybe
will say of me in the years to come:

forgive his moods – was the momentum
bitterness that made him write?
He was wholly on the side of freedom,
he was wholly on the side of light!

5 February 1914

88

As the Ocean Changes Colour

As the ocean changes colour
when mountainous cloud alps form
and light erupts from a crater –
so the heart in the singing storm
changes its shape, fears to breathe in,
and colour floods into the face,
and the heart constricts with happiness,
before the appearance of Carmen.

4 March 1914

Among the admirers of Carmen, all
that hurrying colourful crowd
often calling her name aloud,
one, like a shadow by the wall
of Lillas Pastia's bar at night,
stays silent, watches sombrely,
does not wait seeking sympathy,
but when the tambourine is hit
and bangles clash together, he
remembers the April sunlight,
he, under a furious storm
of chords, watches her singing form
and sees the poems he must write.

26 March 1914

Shamelessly, Endlessly Sinning

Shamelessly, endlessly sinning;
losing count of the nights and days
and, with a head from liquor spinning,
creeping into church under God's gaze.

Three times making obeisance,
seven times the sign of the cross,
in secret touching the paving
with a forehead like a furnace.

Into the plate putting a copper;
three times, seven times planting a kiss
on a tawdry icon's border
worn with the ages' lip-service.

Then, no sooner home than cheating
someone out of that coin in the plate
and with a hiccup booting, beating
a starving mongrel from the gate.

Under the lamp by the icon
drinking tea and totting up figures.
Then thumbing through counterfoils taken
from a fat-bellied chest of drawers,

and on a bed's down-quilted cover
collapsing with a sullen snore . . .
Yes, even as you are, my Russia,
I love no other country more.

26 August 1914

Those born in the years of stagnation
forget now how they found their way.
We – children of Russia's tribulation –
forget not a year, not a day.

What message, years of conflagration,
have you: madness or hope? On thin
cheeks strained by war and liberation
bloody reflections still remain.

Dumbness remains – alarm bells clanging
have clapped all other tongues in chains.
In hearts, familiar once with singing,
a fateful emptiness remains.

And what if dark above our death-bed,
cawing, the ravens climb –
Let those more worthy, God, O God,
see your kingdom in their time.

8 September 1914

The Kite

Describing circle after circle
a wheeling kite scans a field
lying desolate. In her hovel
a mother's wailing to her child:
'Come, take my breast, boy, feed on this,
grow, know your place, shoulder the cross.'

Centuries pass, villages flame,
are stunned by war and civil war.
My country, you are still the same,
tragic, beautiful as before.
How long must the mother wail?
How long must the kite wheel?

22 March 1916

I

Darkness – and white
snow hurled
by the wind. The wind!
You cannot stand upright
for the wind: the wind
scouring God's world.

The wind ruffles
the white snow, pulls
that treacherous
wool over the wicked ice.
Everyone out walking
slips. Look – poor thing!

From building to building over
the street a rope skips nimbly,
a banner on the rope – ALL POWER
TO THE CONSTITUENT ASSEMBLY.
This old weeping woman is worried to death,
she doesn't know what it's all about:
that banner – for God's sake –
so many yards of cloth!
How many children's leggings it would make –
and they without shirts – without boots – without . . .

The old girl like a puffed hen picks
her way between drifts of snow.
'Mother of God, these Bolsheviks
will be the death of us, I know!'

Will the frost never lose its grip
or the wind lay its whips aside?
The bourgeois where the roads divide
stands chin on chest, his collar up.

But who's this with the mane
of hair, saying in a
whisper: 'They've sold us down
the river. Russia's down and out.'?
A pen-pusher, no doubt,
a word-spinner . . .

There's someone in a long coat, sidling
over there where the snow's less thick.
What's happened to your joyful tidings,
Comrade cleric?

Do you remember the old days:
waddling belly-first to prayer,
when the cross on your belly would blaze
on the faithful there?

A lady in a fur
is turning to a friend:
'We cried our eyes out, dear . . .'
She slips up –
smack! – on her beam end.

Heave ho
and up she rises – so!

The wind rejoices,
mischievous and spry,
ballooning dresses
and skittling passers-by.
It buffets with a shower
of snow the banner-cloth: ALL POWER
TO THE CONSTITUENT ASSEMBLY,
and carries voices.

. . . Us girls had a session . . .
. . . in there on the right . . .
. . . had a discussion . . .
. . . carried a motion . . .
ten for a time, twenty-five for the night . . .
and not a rouble less
from anybody . . . coming up . . . ?

Evening ebbs out.
The crowds decamp.
Only a tramp
potters about.
And the wind screams . . .

Hey you! Hey
chum,
going my way . . . ?

A crust!
What will become
of us? Get lost!

Black sky grows blacker.

Anger, sorrowful anger
seethes in the breast . . .
Black anger, holy anger . . .

Friend!
Keep your eyes skinned!

II

The wind plays up: snow flutters down.
Twelve men are marching through the town.

Their rifle-butts on black slings sway.
Lights left, right, left, wink all the way . . .

Cap tilted, fag drooping, every one
looks like a jailbird on the run.

Freedom, freedom,
down with the cross!

Rat-a-tat-tat!

It's cold, boys, and I'm numb!

'Johnny and Kate are living it up . . .'
'She's banknotes in her stocking-top.'

'John's in the money, too, and how!'
'He *was* one of us; he's gone over now!'

'Well, mister John, you son of a whore,
just you kiss my girl once more!'

Freedom, freedom,
down with the cross!
Johnny right now is busy with Kate.
What do you think they're busy at?

Rat-a-tat-tat!

Lights left, right, left, lights all the way . . .
Rifles on their shoulders sway . . .

Keep A Revolutionary Step!
The Relentless Enemy Will Not Stop!

Grip your gun like a man, brother!
Let's have a crack at Holy Russia,
Mother
Russia
with her big fat arse!
Freedom, freedom! Down with the cross!

III

The lads have all gone to the wars
to serve in the Red Guard –
to serve in the Red Guard –
and risk their hot heads for the cause.

Hell and damnation,
life is such fun
with a ragged greatcoat
and a Jerry gun!

To smoke the nobs out of their holes
we'll light a fire through all the world,
a bloody fire through all the world –
Lord, bless our souls!

IV

The blizzard whirls; a cabby shouts;
away fly Johnny and Kate
with a 'lectric lamp
between the shafts . . .
Hey there, look out!

He's in an Army overcoat,
a silly grin upon his snout.
He's twirling a moustachio,
twirling it about,
joking as they go . . .

Young Johnny's a mighty lover
with a gift of the gab that charms!
He takes her in his arms,
he's talking her over . . .

She throws her head back as they hug
and her teeth are white as pearl . . .
Ah, Kate, my Katey girl,
with your little round mug!

V

Across your collar-bone, my Kate,
a knife has scarred the flesh;
and there below your bosom, Kate,
that little scratch is fresh!

Hey there, honey, honey, what
a lovely pair of legs you've got!

You carried on in lace and furs –
carry on, dear, while you can!
You frisked about with officers –
frisk about, dear, while you can!

Honey, honey, swing your skirt!
My heart is knocking at my shirt!

Do you remember that officer –
the knife put an end to him . . .
Do you remember that, you whore,
or does your memory dim?

Honey, honey, let him be!
You've got room in bed for me!

Once upon a time you wore grey spats,
scoffed chocolates in gold foil,
went out with officer-cadets –
now it's the rank and file!

Honey, honey, don't be cruel!
Roll with me to ease your soul!

VI

Carriage again and cabby's shout
come storming past: 'Look out! Look out!'

Stop, you, stop! Help, Andy – here!
Cut them off, Peter, from the rear!

Crack – crack – reload – crack – crack – reload!
The snow whirls skyward off the road.

Young Johnny and the cabman run
like the wind. Take him. Give them one

for the road. Crack – crack! Now learn
.   .   .   .
to leave another man's girl alone!

Running away, you bastard? Do.
Tomorrow I'll settle accounts with you!

But where is Kate? She's dead! She's dead!
A bullet hole clean through her head!

Kate, are you satisfied? Lost your tongue?
Lie in the snow-drift then, like dung!

Keep A Revolutionary Step!
The Relentless Enemy Will Not Stop!

VII

Onward the twelve advance,
their butts swinging together,
but the poor killer looks
at the end of his tether . . .

Fast, faster, he steps out.
Knotting a handkerchief
clumsily round his throat
his hand shakes like a leaf . . .

'What's eating you, my friend?'
'Why so downhearted, mate?'
'Come, Pete, what's on your mind?
Still sorry for Kate?'

'Oh, brother, brother, brother,
I loved that girl . . .
such nights we had together,
me and that girl . . .
For the wicked come-hither
her eyes would shoot at me,
and for the crimson mole
in the crook of her arm,
I shot her in my fury –
like the fool I am . . .'

'Hey, Peter, shut your trap!'
'Are you a woman or
are you a man, to pour
your heart out like a tap?'
'Hold your head up
and take a grip!'

'This isn't the time now
for me to be your nurse!
Brother, tomorrow
will be ten times worse!'

And shortening his stride,
slowing his step,
Peter lifts his head
and brightens up . . .

What the hell!
It's not a sin to have some fun!

Put your shutters up, I say –
There'll be broken locks today!

Open your cellars: quick, run down . . . !
The scum of the earth are hitting the town!

VIII

My God, what a life!
I've had enough!
I'm bored!

I'll scratch my head
and dream a dream . . .

I'll chew my quid
to pass the time . . .

I'll swig enough
to kill my drought . . .

I'll get a knife
and slit your throat!

Fly away, mister, like a starling,
before I drink your blue veins dry
for the sake of my poor darling
with her dark and roving eye . . .

Blessed are the dead which die in the Lord . . .

I'm bored!

IX

Out of the city spills no noise,
the prison tower reigns in peace.
We've got no booze but cheer up, boys,
we've seen the last of the police!

The bourgeois where the roads divide
stands chin on chest, his collar up:
mangy and flea-bitten at his side
shivers a coarse-haired mongrel pup.

The bourgeois with a hangdog air
stands speechless, like a question mark,
and the old world behind him there
stands with its tail down in the dark.

X

Still the storm rages gust upon gust.
What weather! What a storm!
At arm's length you can only just
make out your neighbour's form.

Snow twists into a funnel,
a towering tunnel . . .

'Oh, what a blizzard! . . . Jesus Christ!'
'Watch it, Pete, cut out that rot!
What did Christ and his bloody cross
ever do for the likes of us?
Look at your hands. Aren't they hot
with the blood of the girl you shot?'

Keep A Revolutionary Step!
The Enemy Is Near And Won't Let Up!

Forward, and forward again
the working men!

XI

Abusing God's name as they go,
all twelve march onward into snow . . .
prepared for anything,
regretting nothing . . .

Their rifles at the ready
for the unseen enemy
in back streets, side roads
where only snow explodes
its shrapnel, and through quag-
mire drifts where the boots drag . . .

before their eyes
throbs a red flag.

Left, right,
the echo replies.

Keep your eyes skinned
lest the enemy strike!

Into their faces day and night
bellows the wind
without a break . . .

Forward, and forward again
the working men!

XII

. . . On they march with sovereign tread . . .
'Who else goes there? Come out! I said
come out!' It is the wind and the red
flag plunging gaily at their head.

The frozen snow-drift looms in front.
'Who's in the drift! Come out! Come here!'
There's only the homeless mongrel runt
limping wretchedly in the rear . . .

'You mangy beast, out of the way
before you taste my bayonet.
Old mongrel world, clear off I say!
I'll have your hide to sole my boot!'

The shivering cur, the mongrel cur
bares his teeth like a hungry wolf,
droops his tail, but does not stir . . .
'Hey, answer, you there, show yourself.'

'Who's that waving the red flag?'
'Try and see! It's as dark as the tomb!'
'Who's that moving at a jog
trot, keeping to the back-street gloom?'

'Don't you worry – I'll catch you yet;
better surrender to me alive!'
'Come out, comrade, or you'll regret
it – we'll fire when I've counted five!'

Crack – crack – crack! But only the echo
answers from among the eaves . . .
The blizzard splits his seams, the snow
laughs wildly up the whirlwind's sleeve . . .

Crack – crack – crack!
Crack – crack – crack!

. . . So they march with sovereign tread . . .
Behind them limps the hungry dog,
and wrapped in wild snow at their head
carrying a blood-red flag –
soft-footed where the blizzard swirls,
invulnerable where bullets crossed –
crowned with a crown of snowflake pearls,
a flowery diadem of frost,
ahead of them goes Jesus Christ.

January 1918

The Scythians

> Panmongolism! Uncouth name,
> but music to my ear.
>
> *Vladimir Solovyov*

You have millions. We are numberless,
numberless, numberless. Try doing
battle with us! Yes, we are Scythians! Yes,
Asiatics, with greedy eyes slanting!

For you, the centuries; for us, one hour.
We, like obedient lackeys, have held up
a shield dividing two embattled powers –
the Mongol hordes and Europe!

For centuries your furnaces have bellowed
and drowned the avalanche's thunder.
And a strange tale it seemed to you, the loud
collapse of Lisbon and Messina!

The West for centuries has looked our way,
absorbed our pearls into its profits.
Derisively you waited for the day
when you could hold us in your cannon sights.

Now the day dawns. Disaster spreads its wings,
and insults gather to a head.
The day may follow whose sun rising brings
no shadow where your Paestums stood.

Old world, before your ancient splendour sinks –
all-wise one, suffering sweet torment –
like Oedipus before the riddling Sphinx
pause and consider for a moment.

Russia is a Sphinx. Grieving, jubilant,
and covering herself with blood
she looks, she looks, she looks at you – her slant
eyes lit with hatred and with love.

Yes – love. For centuries you have not known
such love as sets our hot blood churning.
You have forgotten that the world has shown
love can devastate with its burning!

All things we love – the mystic's divine gift,
the fever of cold calculus;
all we appreciate – the Frenchman's shaft
of wit, the German's genius . . .

and we remember all things – hellhole streets
of Paris, cool Venetian stone,
lemon groves far off, fragrant in the heat,
and smoky pinnacles of Cologne . . .

We love the flesh, its colour and its taste,
its suffocating mortal odour . . .
Are we to blame if your rib-cages burst
beneath our paws' impulsive ardour?

We have grown accustomed – seizing mane
and halter, wrestling with a rope –
to breaking in wild horses to the rein,
and taming slave-girls to our grip.

Come to us – from your battlefield nightmares
into our peaceful arms! While there's
still time, hammer your swords into ploughshares,
friends, comrades! We shall be brothers!

If you do not, we have nothing to lose.
Our faith, too, can be broken.
You will be cursed for centuries, centuries,
by your descendants' sickly children!

We shall take to the wilds and the mountain
woods, letting beautiful Europe through,
and as we move into the wings shall turn
an asiatic mask to you.

March all together, march to the Urals!
We clear the ground for when the armoured
juggernauts with murder in their sights
meet the charge of the mongol horde.

We shall ourselves no longer be your shield,
no longer launch our battlecries;
but study the convulsive battlefield
from far off through our narrow eyes!

We shall not stir when the murderous Huns
pillage the dead, turn towns to ash,
in country churches stable their squadrons,
and foul the air with roasting flesh.

Now, for the last time, see the light, old world!
To peace and brotherhood and labour –
our bright feast – for the last time you are called
by the strings of a Scythian lyre!

30 January 1918

Notes

The poems are arranged in chronological order, with one or two
exceptions: the 'Dances of Death', for example, are all grouped
together. Blok usually dated his poems carefully, and the dates given
are those of the Julian calendar, which was used in pre-Revolutionary
Russia. Where the poem was worked on over a number of years, the
first date only is given. The division into three books is that made by
Blok himself.

'A RED GLOW IN THE SKY'
In his notebooks for 1918 Blok recalls how the pinewoods near
Shakhmatovo appeared to him at evening like the silhouette of an
ancient city. The 'roar' of the next-to-last line is a recurring word in
Blok's writing; he uses the same word to describe his perception of the
Revolution of 1917.

'I SEEK SALVATION'
The first appearance in Blok's poems of the Beautiful Lady, who is
always addressed in the intimate or religious second person singular
(French *tu*) and always with a capital letter.

'THE INTELLECT CANNOT MEASURE THE DIVINE'
Blok once described the Russian Venus as a 'strange form' of the
Beautiful Lady – a hint of the importance Russia was later to assume
in his poems. In the same way the 'different warriors' of the last stanza
seem to prefigure the Red Guards of *The Twelve* (see p. 94).

'I SENSE YOUR COMING'
In 1901 Blok discovered the poems and philosophy of Vladimir
Solovyov, whose cult of Sophia, the divine wisdom, had a great influ-
ence on the expression of Blok's mystical vision. The 'change of shape'
looks forward to the various spectres who later took the place of the
Lady (the Stranger, the Snow Maiden, etc.)

'I ENTER THE DARK CHURCH SLOWLY'
Written shortly before Lyubov agreed to marry Blok.

'THE FACTORY'
The censors did not at first allow this poem to be published; it marks

more or less the first appearance in Blok's poems of a social theme. The colour yellow always has repulsive connotations for him; it is usually associated with the soulless meanness of modern industrial civilization.

'INTRODUCTION TO THE SECOND BOOK OF POEMS'
Originally entitled 'Prayer'; the poem is addressed to the Beautiful Lady and was first printed as an Introduction to Book Two in 1916.

'ILLUSION'
From a group of St Petersburg poems entitled *The City*. Blok wrote in a letter three days after finishing this poem: 'I am writing poems with long lines, sometimes quite excessively long, but still I like them better than my previous poems; they seem stronger. Don't reproach me with this excess; through it I am expressing *just the same thing* as in the previous "vague" poems, but in the form of shouts, insanity and frequently excruciating dissonances.'

'THE LITTLE PRIEST OF THE FEN'
From a group of poems entitled *Earth's Bubbles*; see *Macbeth* I. iii: 'The earth hath bubbles, as the water has, and these are of them'. Blok wrote of these poems: 'The waking earth brings little shaggy creatures out to the edges of the woods. All they can do is to shout "Goodbye" to the winter, caper about and tease passers-by.'

'AUTUMN FREEDOM'
Almost the first appearance of one of Blok's major themes, the open road of drunken Russia, with the blizzard, the wind, and the freedom of the beggar-poet, escaping from the living death and the desperate illusions of the City.

'A GIRL WAS SINGING'
Ships sailing into harbour were always a powerful image of recovered happiness for Blok, particularly in 1905–6. See later the poem *Do You Remember* (p. 77) and the fourth section of *Retribution* (p. 73).

'THE STRANGER'
Another poem from *The City*: the scene is a station buffet in the suburbs of St Petersburg. Blok was indignant with critics who saw in the Stranger simply a reincarnation of the Beautiful Lady. For all her heady charm she is in fact a vision induced by wine and the smoke of locomotives, a beautiful doll who impersonates the Beautiful Lady and

mocks the poet's inability to distinguish between dreams and reality, good and evil. In a later essay Blok describes her as 'a diabolical fusion from many worlds, mainly the blue and the lilac'. In other poems and in a verse drama she appears as a falling (or fallen) star.

'RUSSIA'
Russia is always a woman in Blok's poems; here she is a complex figure, at the same time poor gypsy girl, sleeping princess, and mother. Much of the material for this poem came from Blok's work for an article on the poetry of spells and charms.

'SNOW WINE'
This and the next four poems were inspired by the actress N.N. Volokhova, a member of the company directed by Meyerhold, which gave the first performance of Blok's play *The Puppet Show*. The first two are from a cycle of thirty poems *The Snow Mask*, written in the space of a fortnight and dominated by the snowstorm, the falling star (or comet), the intoxication of wine and dance, and the unreality of the masquerade.

'CAUGHT BY THE BLIZZARD'
The 'fallen tsar' of the last line is the heart's sun, which may still rise in a new dawn.

'O SPRING WITHOUT END'
This and the next two poems come from another cycle, *Oath by Fire and Darkness*. Here the masquerade and blizzard give way to a theme which was to remain with Blok, the gypsy dance leading out to the open spaces of Russia.

'SHE CAME IN FROM THE FROST'
Again inspired by N.N. Volokhova, this is almost Blok's only poem in free verse. He loved *Macbeth* and used the passage about 'earth's bubbles' (I. iii) as an epigraph to a section of Book Two. The story of Paolo and Francesca is in Dante's *Inferno*, Canto V.

'ON THE FIELD OF KULIKOVO'
At the battle of Kulikovo, fought in 1380 between the River Don and the river Nepryadva, the Russian forces under Prince Dmitry Donskoi defeated the Tartar army (the Horde) led by Khan Mamai. For Blok this heroic struggle was a portent of Russia's immediate future, in which bloodshed and suffering would give birth to a new order. The

'white stone' of the second poem is the magical stone Alatir of Russian folk-legend.

'RUSSIA'

The notion of Russia as a woman (gypsy? princess? peasant?) held captive by the charms of a magician (the successive governments of Russia) recurs in many of Blok's poems (for example, *Russia*, p.37, and *Retribution*, p. 71).

'I AM NAILED TO A BAR'

The troika image (see also the previous poem) inevitably evokes for Russian readers Gogol's vision of Russia as a galloping troika. Blok developed this theme in 1908 in a memorable paper about the intelligentsia and the people, where he sees the intellectual and governing elite of Russia as overshadowed by the rapidly looming troika of the real Russia (the 150 millions).

'CHIVALRY'

Addressed to Blok's wife Lyubov at the end of a year in which they had been virtually separated. But it is also a poem to the Beautiful Lady; in the original version the 'you' of ll. 12–14 was spelt with a capital letter.

'THEY DO NOT TRADE, SLEEP, OR REMEMBER'

Blok wrote to his mother in 1908: 'These two great Christian festivals [Christmas and Easter] depress me more and more; it's as if something was going on, to which I was bitterly hostile.' The last two lines refer to the night in 1902 when Lyubov agreed to be his wife.

'RAVENNA'

Blok later wrote of this poem: 'In Ravenna and round about lie the remains of Theodoric, Dante and the woman who is called Galla in the fourth stanza and Placidia in the fifth. . . . May the archaeologists forgive me my private thoughts about this famous Empress of the fifth century, sister, wife and mother of Roman Emperors and widow of the leader of the Ostrogoths. . . . A medieval tradition has it that she is buried in a seated position, but her high sarcophagus, like those of her son and her husband, is empty. Classe, which lies to the south-east of Ravenna, was a principal Roman port in the time of Augustus, but the Adriatic has long ago receded from these shores and the once bustling port is now no more than a few little houses and the huge half-empty Basilica containing the remains of the holy martyr Apollinarius.'

Dante's *Vita Nuova*, which brings hope of a resurgence of life at the end of the poem, was connected in Blok's mind with his youthful cult of the Beautiful Lady.

'FLORENCE'
Unlike Ravenna, Florence disappointed Blok; it symbolized for him the decadence of Western culture. In a letter to his mother he wrote: 'I curse Florence not only because of the heat and the mosquitoes, but because she has given herself over to European corruption, has become a chattering town and has mutilated nearly all her houses and streets. All that is left is a few palaces, churches and museums, a few distant suburbs and the Boboli gardens – the remaining dust I shake from my feet and wish it the fate of Messina [i.e. earthquake]'. The Beato of the first poem is the painter Fra Angelico. The lily was the emblem of Renaissance Florence. The last poem makes clear the connection in Blok's mind between the fate of Florence and his own life.

'RUSSIA AND I'
Blok's Asiatic vision of Russia in this poem foreshadows *The Scythians*. The Cossack Yermak was one of the conquerors of Siberia in the sixteenth century. The Chud and the Merya were tribes of Central Russia.

'A VOICE FROM THE CHORUS'
Blok once said of this poem: 'A very unpleasant poem. I don't know why I wrote it. It would have been better to leave those words unspoken. But I had to say them. Difficulties have to be overcome. And then will come a fine day.' The original draft was more optimistic than the final version, which was completed in 1914. The connection between this poem and Blok's gypsy lyricism can be seen in a letter of 1912 where he writes: 'My soul imitates the gypsy soul, its wildness and its harmony, and I too sing in a sort of chorus which I shall never leave.' The 'quieter than water now, lower than grass' of the last stanza is a popular saying about the need to live humbly.

'THE COMMANDER'S FOOTSTEPS'
In Don Juan's betrayal of Donna Anna Blok finds a symbol of his own 'betrayal' of the Beautiful Lady. Many of Blok's contemporaries were shocked by the motor-car horn which is the voice of Fate.

'RETRIBUTION'
In 1910 and 1911 Blok made a vigorous effort to break out of his isolated lyricism into a more positive, active, and social life. In particular,

in *Retribution*, modelling himself largely on Pushkin, he set himself to write a long 'classical' poem in iambic meter which would set his own private fate and that of his father in the perspective of Russian history between 1880 and 1910 – a sort of Rougon-Macquart epic he called it. The poem was never completed; this extract was to have been the historical introduction to the second of three main chapters. In it Blok evokes the reactionary period following the assassination of Tsar Alexander II in 1881, a period dominated by the Procurator of the Holy Synod, Pobedonostsev. The first part takes up the image of Russia as a sleeping beauty under a magician's spell which appeared earlier in the poem *Russia* (p. 37). The Tsar of Part III is Alexander III. The last two lines refer to the Russo-Japanese war and the Revolution of 1905.

'YES. THIS IS THE CALL OF INSPIRATION'
Another poem inspired in part by Blok's trip to Western Europe in the summer of 1911. Like the following poem, it seems originally to have been intended for the long poem *Retribution* but was eventually included in a group of fierce short poems entitled *Iambs*.

'DO YOU REMEMBER'
In 1911 Blok and his wife stayed at Aber' Wrach in Brittany. In a letter to his mother he recounts the arrival of the four warships, which he interpreted as a sign of the impending European war.

'DANCES OF DEATH'
These five poems, like the poems on pp. 67, 68, 84, and 85, were included in a section of Blok's collected poems entitled *Terrible World*. The first poem may have been inspired by a contemporary journalist, but it also recalls Blok's preoccupation with the living death of the artist. The last poem, with its popular-song rhythm and its menacing new tsar, anticipates *The Twelve*.

'THE IMPULSES OF YOUTH'
Blok was much preoccupied with the loss of happiness which had accompanied his descent from the heaven of the Beautiful Lady into the hell of art (see, for instance, *To the Muse*). This poem records one of the rare moments in a bleak period when the satisfactions of poetry outweighed for him his personal unhappiness.

'WORLDS FLY PAST'
Blok often compared his life to a flight over the abyss. The flight could

be intoxicating, as in *The Snow Mask*, but more often it was nerve-racking and exhausting.

'TO THE MUSE'
Blok put this poem at the beginning of his third book; it sums up his feelings about the 'hell' of art. The Muse is as much of a degeneration from the Beautiful Lady as the Stranger or the Snow Maiden. In his article 'On the Present State of Russian Symbolism' he wrote: 'In the dark air of Hell lives the artist who has glimpsed other worlds. When the golden sword is quenched . . . there is a confusion of worlds and the artist in the deep midnight of art goes mad and dies.'

'THE ARTIST'
Another expression of Blok's high Romantic attitude to poetry, akin to Tyutchev's famous line: 'Your thought when spoken is a lie'. In 'On the Present State of Russian Symbolism' he shows the poet conjuring with life only to possess a doll, the doll which has replaced the once living Beautiful Lady.

'I WANT TO LIVE'
The first poem in the section *Iambs*, preceded by a dedication to Blok's dead half-sister and an epigraph from Juvenal: 'Fecit indignatio versum'.

'AS THE OCEAN CHANGES COLOUR'
This and the following poem are from the cycle *Carmen*, addressed to the opera-singer L.A. Delmas, whom Blok first saw in the role of Carmen.

'SHAMELESSLY, ENDLESSLY SINNING'
Originally entitled 'Russia'.

'THOSE BORN IN THE YEARS OF STAGNATION'
Written just after the outbreak of the First World War. The 'years of stagnation' are the period of reaction evoked in the passage from *Retribution* on p. 71. The terrible 'years of conflagration' had seen the Russo-Japanese war (l. 7 of this poem) and now the outbreak of what Blok both welcomed and feared as the purifying cataclysm. In the third stanza he applies to his whole generation the same words (fateful emptiness') which he used so often to describe his own state; very clearly here we see the poet-prophet.

'THE KITE'

One of Blok's last short poems, this was adapted from a rough draft for the first Chapter of *Retribution*, where the images of the hawk of disaster and grieving mother-Russia also appear.

'THE TWELVE'

Written in a period of a few days in January 1918; on finishing it Blok wrote in his notebook: 'Today I am a genius.' For a discussion of this poem see the Introduction. The Constituent Assembly was a body set up by the Provisional Government which came to power in March 1917. It was dispersed by the Bolsheviks on 6 January 1918, the day after its first meeting.

'THE SCYTHIANS'

Written immediately after *The Twelve*, at a time when the Soviet Government was negotiating with Germany at Brest-Litovsk, this is a plea to the Western Powers to respond to Russia's call for peace and friendship. For Blok, Russia's historic role had been to stand as a shield between the West and the 'yellow peril'. But Russia had her Asiatic side (see also *Russia*, p. 37); if the Revolution was rejected by the West she could unleash the destructive anti-cultural forces which the word Asia signified. Blok's diary for 11 January 1918 contains the words: 'If you do not wash off the shame of your wartime patriotism with at least a "democratic peace", if you wreck our revolution, it means that you are *no longer Aryans*. And we shall open wide the Eastern Gates. We looked at you with the eyes of Aryans as long as you had a face. But we shall peer at your muzzle with our *squint-eyed*, cunning, rapid look; we shall turn into Asiatics and the East will flood over you.'

The third stanza refers to the earthquakes of Lisbon (1755) and Messina (1908). The second of these had seemed to Blok a portent of the imminent collapse of modern industrial civilization which had for so long denied the Spirit of Music and the elements.

Chronology of Blok's Life

1880	Aleksandr Aleksandrovich Blok born in St Petersburg
1889	Blok's parents divorced: his mother remarries
1891	Blok enters High School in St Petersburg
1898	Enters St Petersburg university, Faculty of Law
	Beginning of love for L.D. Mendeleeva
1901	Discovers writings of Vladimir Solovyov; 'mystical summer'
	Transfers to Faculty of Letters
1903	First poems published in a literary magazine
	Marriage with L.D. Mendeleeva
1904	Publication of *Poems about the Beautiful Lady*
1905	Carries a red flag in the Revolution
1906	Leaves the university
	Publication of second collection of poems and several articles.
	Publication and production of his first play, *The Puppet Show*
1907	Love affair with N.N. Volokhova
	Publication of *The Snow Mask*
1908	Publication of another volume of poems and a collection of lyrical plays
	Lectures and articles on social themes
	Composition of 'On the Field of Kulikovo'
1909	Visit to Italy and Germany, with his wife
	Visit to Warsaw, where his father dies
1910	Important lecture 'On the Present State of Russian Symbolism
1911	Composition of *Retribution*
	Visits Western Europe
1911–12	Publication of collected poems in three volumes
1913	Visits France and the Basque country
	Finishes his play, *The Rose and the Cross*
1914	Love affair with L.A. Delmas
1916–17	Serves as a soldier in the Pinsk marshes
1917	Return to Petrograd after the February Revolution
	Works on the commission investigating the Tsarist government
1918	Composition of *The Twelve* and *The Scythians*
	Prepares final edition of his collected poems in three volumes
1918–21	Constant official activity in connection with literature and the theatre
1921	Blok dies after a long and painful illness